Understanding Looked After Children

An Introduction to Psychology for Foster Care

Jeune Guishard-Pine, Suzanne McCall and Lloyd Hamilton

Foreword by Andrew Wiener

Jessica Kingsley Publishers
London and Philadelphia

First published in 2007
by Jessica Kingsley Publishers
116 Pentonville Road
London N1 9JB, UK
and
400 Market Street, Suite 400
Philadelphia, PA 19106, USA

www.jkp.com

Library of Congress Cataloging in Publication Data
A CIP catalog record for this book is available from the Library of Congress

British Library Cataloguing in Publication Data
A CIP catalogue record for this book is available from the British Library

ISBN 978 1 84310 370 7

Printed and bound in Great Britain by
Athenaeum Press, Gateshead, Tyne and Wear

Contents

Foreword

Being a foster carer is a rewarding and challenging experience. It is increasingly recognised that a period of safe, secure and stable family life can be deeply healing for a child who has been deprived of these things in their birth family. Some children can adjust to the fostering experience better than others. Some lap up the opportunity for fun and joy, warmth and comfort, and thrive in their foster family. Some find the experience more challenging. They may have learned that things that appear good can easily turn bad, or that it is dangerous to trust adults. Children cannot 'snap out' of this frame of mind – they have formed these attitudes through bitter experience. Only gradually, over a number of years, can they learn that the world is a better place than they thought it was. This realisation can permanently change the course of a young person's life and help them form secure, loving relationships in adulthood, and make healthy choices about education, work and lifestyle.

Such children present a challenge not just to foster carers, but to the community, social workers, schools and health professionals – but the rewards of success are high. The government has risen to the challenge by calling for foster carers to become more professional, and to have more parental authority and more support, training and supervision. This will enable foster carers to be better equipped to support looked after children in their path to recovery. The challenge to foster carers is to assimilate the skills and attitudes that will enable them to be truly professional carers.

Foster carers deserve a huge amount of respect; there are many people who do not have the skills and ability to take on this task. In my work, working closely with Camden Social Services, I know that skilled foster carers can be the key that enables a young person to achieve health and well-being, and foster carers help me tremendously in my task of trying to understand and assist children.

This book is a very helpful resource for foster carers who are taking up this challenge for the first time, or who are already experienced foster carers. The strength of this book is that the authors speak from years of experience of working with carers and children, and present in simple terms the psychological theoretical frameworks that help us think about and understand looked after children. They also provide practical advice for approaching some of the difficulties looked after children present, and demystify the process of becoming a foster carer.

Dr Andrew Wiener
Consultant Child and Adolescent Psychiatrist
Tavistock Clinic and Camden Multi-Agency Liaison Team

Acknowledgements

The writing of this book has been an enormous adventure...an odyssey even! There has been so much that has been unexpected, yet wonderful. We would first of all like to thank each other for the expertise that has spawned the ideas presented in this book – it has been a mutually inspirational experience. We would like to thank our families and dear, dear friends for their patience in allowing us to be physically present, but emotionally absent. We would like to thank our publishers for sharing in this experience with us. We would like to thank the Bedfordshire and Luton Mental Health and Social Care Partnership Trust for creating this opportunity through the bold and insightful thinking that established the Luton Family Consultation Clinic's Service to Children Requiring Intensive Psychological Therapies (SCRIPT). Special thanks and gratitude to Dr Siobain Maguire for agreeing to conduct her pioneering research with us and thereby enhancing our professional relationships and reputation with the Luton Social Services Department; and also to Mrs Rebecca Collett for her flawless administrative support. We are grateful to Dr Andy Wiener for taking the time to read the first draft of this book. Last but not least, we would like to thank the foster carers and the Luton Family Placement team for their commitment and sheer professionalism in sharing with us their thoughts about, and observations of, the vulnerable children that we serve.

How to Read this Book

We know very well that the readers will have different expectations and want different things from this book. The heading 'How to Read this Book' is not an attempt to tell the reader how to approach it, but rather we thought it worthwhile to very briefly explain some intentional aspects of the book's shape and form that may differ from the 'usual' for such an introductory text.

The first difference may be experienced as the different 'voices' or styles of writing from chapter to chapter. Each of the three authors has written at least three chapters in this book, and while we have been careful to avoid *too* much variation in style, we have preserved the individuality (personality and professional/theoretical background) of each author. If you like, we considered it important to let readers experience some difference: unlike milk, we have not become 'homogenised'!

The main thinking behind this is that we feel that it accurately reflects the world of multidisciplinary thinking that surrounds children who are looked after, and which therefore will be part of the foster carer's experience. For example, child-in-care reviews and case conferences are attended by a variety of different professionals, all of whose opinion and thinking is invited. Sometimes this leads to differences in opinion which can be difficult to negotiate in applying the rule that it is the child's best interests that must be considered as paramount. However, multidisciplinary thinking and working is a vital way of representing a variety of options and possibilities and of drawing on a range of valuable opinions and experiences. In this book we also aim to encourage foster carers to see themselves very much in this mix of opinions and expertise, and we hope that the change of 'voices' from chapter to chapter not only introduces the idea of difference, but also encourages readers to have faith in their own contributions in the process of making decisions about the child in their care.

Further related to this is the added layer of the very many different theories and voices that specifically contribute to the discipline of psychology. We have referred to this from time to time in the book: there is no one 'truth' or answer in psychological theory. For this reason too, we have reflected the idea of difference in the style of the book.

The second characteristic of our approach has been to try and write very accessibly, but not to exclude words and ideas that are seen as key in the world of child care and psychology. While mostly we explain these ideas in the text, we have also listed and briefly defined them in the glossary at the back of the book. Glossary terms appear in bold at their first mention in each chapter. We hope that this will prove a useful reference for readers and they then become familiar with some commonly used terms.

Each chapter also has a different pace, by which we mean that in some chapters we have taken much space to explore and think about single or linked ideas (as in Chapter 4), and in other chapters we have been much more brief in presenting wide-ranging concepts about diagnosis and symptoms (as in Chapter 6). We hope that this will broaden the usefulness of the book to the reader.

Finally, you should view the reading of this book as an exciting event within the odyssey that you will doubtlessly experience through fostering.

CHAPTER 1

Introduction

The psychological well-being of children in the care system has been receiving increasing levels of attention due to corresponding increases in research on both the difficulties and the interventions involved in helping those children with mental health needs (Carr 2000). Surveys have consistently shown that the psychological needs of children in the care system are significant, in terms of high levels of arrested physical and psychological development (Roth and Fonagy 2004). Specific research in the UK such as that by Maguire (2005) has also shown with increasing clarity the role that foster families can play in accelerating the child's return to a path of more healthy developmental progress.

There have also been recent discussions of 'professionalising' foster carers (e.g. DfES 2006; Hutchinson, Asquith and Simmonds 2003). This means that other professionals have been looking at developing the knowledge and skills of foster carers in order to enhance their work, given what we now understand to be the costs to individuals and society of not meeting the needs of the increasingly complex and psychologically vulnerable children in foster care. Our background research in writing this book has indicated that, despite this combination of facts, there is still a serious lack of accessible literature available to support foster carers' understanding of the very significant needs of these children, and to contribute to the development of their increasingly specialised role. We hope this book is a first step in a series of developments to address this issue.

In our view, the need for this book has become quite urgent. Many good people are arriving at foster panels with limited understanding of the wide range of needs of looked after children and the possible impact of these needs on themselves and/or their families. This book is essential reading for registered foster carers, and people putting themselves forward for selection as foster carers. It is a book for you to read as early as possible in the process, so that you are more aware of both the fulfilment and the challenges that the role can bring. Every bit of help that foster carers receive to support children is an investment in the children themselves. The book will be useful for adoptive parents, too. It is also expected that it will be useful background reading for both experienced and trainee practitioners in the professional systems of care outlined in the 'protective shield' (see Chapter 2) in understanding their statutory role in supporting children looked after by foster carers, and also supporting the foster carers themselves.

This book will be an essential guide to some of the dominant psychological issues facing looked after children and their carers. It will also discuss the foster carer's ideal role(s) in contributing to the **reparative** and developmental work that needs to be done as an integral part of their task of caring for distressed and vulnerable children. This book has been written to alert you to a wide range of information on the psychological processes that may affect you and your family as well as the foster child. You will also be introduced to the truism that we each seek a sense of 'normalcy'. In our experience, normalcy exists around ideas such as that we all have a desire to reduce anxiety and to increase security; that we all anticipate change as integral to the process of growth; and that we are all part of many social systems, all at the same time. The purpose of sharing this information with you is to increase your awareness and understanding of the psychological issues facing looked after children and how this potentially impacts on foster carers and their families in their unique responsibility as 24-hour support workers with multiple roles (e.g. as biological parent, partner, employee, daughter/son, sibling). The book will describe some of the most prevalent psychological needs of these children and offer guidance on how to support them and also on how to address them in collaboration with other professional partners. For each main concept introduced we will provide a case study or vignette to illustrate the type of needs that characterise the concept. The book will also provide foster carers with language and understanding about the features of stress and distress in children who are placed for child protection reasons, as well as the developmental needs of children with learning difficulties who are placed in foster care to provide **respite** to the biological family.

In our specialised work with foster carers (direct therapeutic/psychological interventions and training), we have found that foster carers often reflect the psychological impact of their relationship with the child(ren) by mirroring powerful feelings of impotence, disappointment and insecurity, or lack of certainty about the future – for example, they express feeling let down, neglected or abandoned by their fostering agency (whether it is their local social services department, or another social services department, or a privately run agency). Although this empathy has some utility, it can become paralysing and disruptive to the necessary collaboration between the carer and the other professional systems. Foster carers can also feel angry with child and adolescent mental health services (**CAMHS**) because of their high-priority agenda of confidentiality. This is often experienced as 'secrecy' and 'obstructive', as foster carers may feel they can only understand the child if they 'know' what the child is saying to the therapist. The skill of the therapist is to attune the foster carer to the needs of the child without breaching confidentiality. Such issues are identified and explored.

Similarly, when a placement breaks down, it is experienced as failure for both the foster carer and the child, and the feelings of loss and rejection percolate through to subsequent placements for both the foster carer and the child. Our work with looked after children gives us a very good indication that the mechanism for reducing the risk of placement breakdown pivots around improving the fit between the foster carers' threshold of tolerance and their understanding and respect for the child's communication of its turmoil. Annexed to this is the hugely important point that the key to foster carers increasing their understanding of children will be accomplished through the parallel process of increasing their self-understanding of the range of feelings that the child evokes in them.

Children who are fostered, especially those who have more enduring problems and mental health needs, are likely to get access to many professionals – social workers, counsellors, teachers, **paediatricians**, nurses, psychologists and even psychiatrists. However, typically these professionals come and go. You may indeed find some answers or some bits of theory or knowledge that enlighten you. However, our belief is that no facts revealed in the pages of this book can be half as helpful as the ideas and concepts that you must actively develop in understanding the children you are fostering now, or go on to foster. In truly understanding their needs you will discover that, as a foster carer, the most valuable tool you have to give a child in your care is yourself.

This book begins by outlining some of the legislative framework around fostering and we introduce the concept of the 'protective shield', which is the network of professional and community-based support that a foster child may have access to (Chapter 2). The cultural, social and legal structures associated with various aspects of foster care and looked after children are described (Chapter 3). Some of the very key theoretical frameworks underlying foster care are then introduced (Chapter 4), allowing you to think through the critical role that foster carers and their families are

expected to play in welcoming children in need into their homes and assisting them on their journey through to psychological health. Chapter 5 is an
orientation to the rich tapestry that foster caring can be. Thinking about
how culture is crucial in the way we all conduct our lives is a vital exercise,
because it becomes so automatic for us within our own families that we
forget how diverse people are in 'the real world'. How is it that you can open
yourself up to the opportunity to welcome and support a child who does not
have the same attitudes, conventions, customs and behaviours that you have?

We then go on to describe the psychological issues that present for so
many looked after children, and give ideas on how you can help children
who have experienced challenges to their physical and psychological development (Chapters 6 and 7). An increasingly non-negotiable aspect of the
foster carer's work is to 'join with' other professional systems that the foster
child is involved in (e.g. education, social services, health), in order to
increase the child's access to the statutory services that have duties to ensure
that the child's wide range of developmental needs are met. Chapter 8
embellishes the idea of the 'protective shield' first introduced in Chapter 2,
and explains why the foster carer is an integral and significant part of that
network of support. We will then introduce you to some of the issues around
the many assessments that foster children may have to experience, the contributions that you may have to make to these, your potential feelings and
attitudes towards these assessments, and the support that you may have to
offer as a consequence of them (Chapter 9). We go on to give you some
insight into your own psychological processes by looking at the feelings you
may be left with when a placement ends, or the potential devastation when a
complaint is made against you or someone in your household (Chapter 10),
or how you might feel about the assessment process for registration as a
foster carer (Chapter 11). Following the conclusion (Chapter 12) you will
find two appendices, a glossary of commonly used terms, and a list of sources
of further information that you may wish to explore.

References

Carr, A. (2000) *What Works with Children and Adolescents? A Critical Review of
Psychological Interventions with Children, Adolescents and their Families.* London:
Routledge.

Department for Education and Skills (DfES) (2006) *Care Matters: Transforming the Lives
of Children and Young People in Care.* London: HMSO.

Hutchinson, B., Asquith, J. and Simmonds, J. (2003) 'Skills protect: Towards a
professional foster care service.' *Adoption and Fostering 3,* 7, 8–13.

Maguire, S. (2005) 'Mental health literacy and attitudes in foster carers: Identification of factors that influence help-seeking.' Unpublished dissertation supervised by J. Guishard-Pine. University of East Anglia.

Roth, A. and Fonagy, P. (2004) *What Works for Whom? A Critical Review of Psychotherapy Research* (2nd edition). Hove: Guilford.

Useful websites

- www.BAAF.co.uk
- www.barnardos.org.uk
- www.familyfutures.co.uk
- www.fostering.net
- www.fostering.org.uk
- www.nch.org.uk

CHAPTER 2

Context

Wherever foster care exists across the world, its function is to provide for the physical, emotional, social and psychological needs of children who for varying reasons can no longer be parented by their mother and/or father or extended family, or whose care needs to be shared, as in **respite** care. Sellick (1999) referred to these vulnerable children as 'social orphans'. This chapter will summarise the growth of foster care in the UK and also draw the reader's attention to global issues around foster care. An account is given of the earliest recorded history of foster care in the UK, and this provides the canvas on which we paint a picture of the developing complexity of the role. The following history is adapted from Ruegger and Rayfield (1999).

The history of foster care in the UK

The earliest records on caring for orphans date back to the 1500s, when they were placed with nurses. By the 1800s a range of institutions (such as Barnardo's) were set up, with the principal aim of meeting the physical needs, but not the social and emotional needs, of **neglected** children. The earliest institutions for neglected or orphaned children were essentially workhouses. The most significant record of fostering as we understand it today was made in 1853, when a child was removed from a workhouse in Cheshire and placed in a foster family under the legal care of the local government. The foster parents were given an allowance by the local government for subsistence, to the value of what the child would have earned in the workhouse. These fostering practices were not wholeheartedly welcomed by the public. The opponents of this method were concerned about a decline in responsible parenting, as it was felt that some parents would neglect their children because they knew that the government would take the responsibility for child rearing away from them. Another fear was that foster carers would house children in exchange for money, but would then go on to mistreat them. As a consequence of such concerns 'boarding-out committees' were formed, with the role of coordinating placements. At the beginning of the 1900s only orphaned or abandoned children under the age of 11 years were fostered, and they had to have an unchallenging psychological profile – well-adjusted, obedient and physically 'normal'.

Until World War II, foster care was seen as a charitable service. Two important events – first the mass evacuation of millions of children, and then the death of a child in care in 1945 – prompted more state intervention, leading to a closer look at foster care practices. Significant research was done by psychologists and psychiatrists, as a direct consequence of the separation of children from their natural parents. This research promoted the importance of close and loving human contact, and it was recognised foremost in John Bowlby's book *Child Care and the Growth of Love* (Bowlby 1953). More is written about Bowlby's work on 'attachment' in Chapter 4.

The popularity of foster care increased, but it was at this time mostly seen as a women's interest, and as such requiring no training. Robertson and Robertson (1969) were the first writers to suggest that foster carers required training on how to successfully meet the child's need to retain a clear sense of family identity and still feel secure in their foster placement. Their work also led to agencies becoming more focused specifically on how to prepare children for changes of placements.

The legal context of foster care in the UK

Today there are about 75,000 children in the care system at any one time in the UK. The number has gradually increased over the last few decades. The Children Act (1989) modernised the professional and administrative systems to improve support for the several thousands of children who were in need of care and protection from neglect, abuses and other threats to their physical and psychological development. (Equivalent legislation to enshrine the principle of child protection exists in most Western countries.) It redefined social work, recommending that professionals must try to support families by working alongside the natural families, as it was felt that keeping the child in their family home was often in their best interests.

Both research and time have shown us that, if a child's psychological development is threatened, placing them in foster care is not a singular or simple solution. Careful consideration needs to be given to this option because of the potential psychological consequences. Family support initially tends to be short-term, intensive support from a social worker or health visitor, or from resources in their local community, such as religious or other voluntary groups. With this help, many families manage to change their style of living so that the child is able to make progress in their development. Many other children and families need specialist help and/or longer periods of time to make effective and lasting changes. Unfortunately, despite the help offered, some of these families are not successful. In the UK, local governments have a duty to ensure that these children do not experience '**significant harm**' (see Chapter 3) as a result of the difficulties their parents or carers have in looking after them.

It is not acceptable for a parent to believe that lack of knowledge of how to provide for the physical and psychological needs of their child justifies neglect or abuse of him or her. This is why the child care systems are designed to unite in their overriding aim of protecting the psychological growth of children in our society. The agency that is most often in contact with the family has a duty to support the child by referring the family to a partner agency that may be able to help them to overcome their difficulties. The interventions offered will take time and resources, and most families manage to benefit from family support work. However, some families do not, and this may mean that their child (or children) are removed to a foster placement where their needs can be better met.

Today Article 20 of the United Nations Convention on the Rights of the Child (see Appendix A) forms the basic principles of modern foster care.

Modern foster care

The place of foster carers in child welfare services has changed considerably over the past two decades. In countries in continental Europe, the overall balance of care is shifting towards less costly and more 'humane' foster care services. This really means less child rearing in institutions. In the UK there is still an emphasis on frequent family contact, on foster care as a voluntary service, and on the importance of social workers, other professional groups, parents and foster carers working together. Time and experience has informed social policy that overall there should be a gradual transfer from residential to foster care, and from child protection to family support programmes. Colton and Williams (1997) defined a quality system for foster caring as comprising the following five main factors.

1.   It may include a structured or unstructured system of care by relatives.

2.   It may arrange placements that are coordinated by a recognised authority.

3. There will be a mixture of temporary and longer-term placements.

4. There will be an expectation of 24-hour care of the child.

5. It will nearly always involve a private household.

As effective child rearing practices have become more refined, the complex nature of fostering has simultaneously come into sharper focus. The indication is that children need a solid idea of who their parents are, as well as who their psychological parent is, in order to achieve personal security that enables them to feel a real sense of permanency and belonging. These hugely important aspects of the child's psychological development have meant that modern foster carers require special skills to support this area of child development, and fostering is beginning to be seen as a professional vocation in acknowledgement of this increased skills repertoire above and beyond that of 'ordinary' parents. In short, modern foster carers need to know what to expect from emotionally, sexually and physically abused children, and how to use specific skills to repair the psychological damage, so that the child can return to a path of more healthy psychological development.

Kinship care

In, for example, Central and Eastern Europe, and also in many African and other developing countries, kinship foster care is one of the commonest and established forms of substitute care for children entering the care system. A study conducted by UNICEF (1997) found that foster children in kinship care often lived with elderly grandparents or other relatives, without adequate financial support. Kinship care is on the increase across the UK. The growth in kinship care is an acknowledgement of the specific benefits of this type of care to foster children. As well as the obvious benefit of increasing placement choice, kinship care greatly assists the child's identity development by reflecting the child's cultural background, consequently lessening the risk of placement breakdown.

Recent developments: the 'professionalisation' of foster carers

Current difficulties in recruiting foster carers are perhaps linked to the fact that within the care system there has been a sharp shift in emphasis towards foster care. In the UK generally we face increasing difficulties in recruiting sufficient numbers of foster carers who are both confident and competent to care, specifically, for children presenting behavioural and emotional difficulties. At the same time, social policy is to reduce highly specialist residential provision for these children. In the UK there is a gradual movement to resourcing foster carers in private agencies in order to meet the need for foster-family care placements. Although the overall number of severely damaged children in the care system has decreased (due to the effectiveness of the social policy to increase family foster care and decrease institutionalised care), there remain significant challenges to local providers concerning appropriate ways of arranging provision and care for such children as do exist.

Although in this culture many parents use some form of corporal punishment with their children on some occasions, this method is not available to those who care for other people's children. Foster carers are expected to behave toward their foster children, not as if they were their own, but increasingly as if they held some professional responsibility towards the child. In practice this means possessing the ability to preserve a sense of distance and objectivity, and still offer the child individual care and concern in the same way as a parent.

The contemporary, 'professional' foster carer is generally thought of as someone whose skills exceed the basic expectations summarised above, and who is paid for possessing the extra skills that are required in order to meet the needs of the most challenging children. The payment of enhanced fees, the expectation of regular training, the provision of respite facilities and specialist advice and support (such as provided by child and adolescent mental health services (**CAMHS**) – see Chapter 6) and a growing recognition, on the part of fostering agencies, of carers as fellow colleagues has contributed to an increasingly 'professional' role for foster carers.

In 2006 the British Government published a Green Paper entitled *Care Matters* which was launched alongside a major consultation process to examine, amongst other factors concerning looked after children, the role of foster care in achieving better outcomes for this vulnerable group of children (DfES 2006). The Green Paper based the case for reform in part on the 'devastating' long-term outcomes for such children, over-represented as they are in a range of vulnerable groups (such as those not in education, teenage parenting, young offenders, drug users and prisoners). The proposals it made regarding foster care included 'introducing a tiered framework for foster placements to respond to different levels of need, underpinned by a new qualifications framework, fee structure and national minimum standards…[and]…extending the use of specialist foster care for children with complex needs' (DfES 2006, p.7). The proposals to 'radically reform the placements system', if seen through, will, it is hoped, increase support and training to foster carers from a variety of agencies, but it is clear that there will be an increased expectation for foster carers to deliver, in partnership with other agencies, better outcomes for the children in their care.

The '**professionalisation**' of foster carers brings with it both pros and cons. Children in the care system tend to be the most troubled and challenging children within a community. It can be argued that working in partnership with parents and exploring ways to support parental care may result in significant delays in the court process for children at risk of significant harm. Although it is usually possible to achieve stability in a foster child's life while the court process is ongoing, the child is likely to have had many disappointments. It may take several years to reverse the psychological effects of prolonged neglect and otherwise inadequate parenting. Modern foster carers have to learn to tolerate and effectively manage challenging and sometimes psychologically disturbed behaviour, while at the same time using overt strategies to enhance the child's self-esteem. Professional foster carers must achieve these aims while maintaining ordinary family life.

In addition to acquiring what are essentially behaviour management skills, the 'professional' foster carers also need to become involved in an expanding range of activities, such as assessing the child's developmental and psychological needs as part of a '**holistic**' approach. They are increasingly required to participate in a range of activities to meet those needs by contributing their intimate knowledge of the child to a network of professionals who are involved in helping the child to maximise his or her potential. In other words, the foster carer must become part of the child's *protective shield* (see Figure 2.1). Further examples of activities of the 'professional' foster carer are: supporting the child in moving on to their next placement; demonstrating skills in writing descriptive reports on the child; court attendance; adopting the role of the '**appropriate adult**'; organising their home for visits from social workers and other professionals; attending and contributing to statutory reviews and planning meetings when required; and being accomplished in the professional language attached to child care, child development and psychological development.

A counsellor the author (Jeune Guishard-Pine) met once described feeling 'safe' as feeling confident. The protective shield is a 'ring of confidence' around a foster child. Figure 2.1 shows the constellation of a support network to promote the healthy psychological development of foster children.

Why do so many people choose to become foster carers?

The reasons why people choose to foster are as varied as the individual life stories of foster carers. The principal reason, however, is that they want to

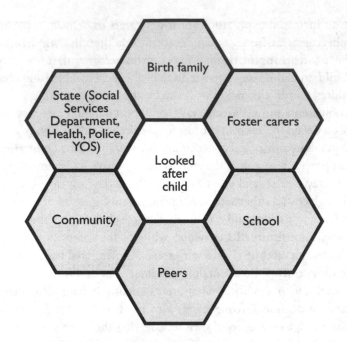

Figure 2.1: A child's protective shield: the ring of confidence

share their lives with children, and choose to support children in need. These children may even be close or distant relatives. There are no longer barriers against fostering by single, co-habiting, same-sex or childless people. Foster carers can also be from diverse social and cultural backgrounds. The main requirements are that you are confident in caring for, listening to, and talking with children, that you are generally fit and healthy, can manage your finances, and that you are willing to learn more about the information and skills required to fulfil your duties as a foster carer confidently and competently. Box 2.1 gives you an idea of the personal challenges that being a foster carer can bring.

The fostering agency will provide a social worker as personal support to you and your family throughout your time as a foster carer. A comprehensive assessment is done by the fostering agency to ensure that you fully understand the task of fostering and how it may affect your family. (See Chapter 11 for more details on the assessment process.)

Specialist foster carers: caring for teenagers

Adolescence can be a significant and much underestimated period of potential disruption to both home and school life. As a transitional period,

---

Box 2.1: Potential psychological and emotional demands in the foster carer–foster child relationship

- Need to have a positive attitude to children's rights and how these may conflict with your own philosophies, opinions, culture, customs and child rearing practices.

- Need to learn how to tolerate being the 'victim' for a while, until the child gains complete trust in you.

- Must recognise that your foster children are likely to have low expectations of adults (particularly those who are close to them) and what they are able to do for them.

- Need to acquire skills for actively building self-esteem and trust in children.

- Need to develop **group management** and **process management** skills.

- Need to understand the concepts of attachment and group dynamics.

- Need to be prepared to develop active listening skills, patience, and a huge capacity for forgiveness.

- Need to become open enough to look deep within yourself, to accept your limitations as a result of factors both outside of and within your control, e.g. needs of your own children or partner, or your own personal history.

- Need to accept and fully own your feelings of guilt and betrayal when foster children move on.

- Need to come to terms with your own physical, emotional and psychological vulnerabilities.

- Need to be fully aware of the **bully–victim cycle**.

(Adapted from Corrick 1996)

---

adolescence has many potentially stressful aspects. While other unsettled behaviour related to the impact of transitional events in a young person's life (e.g. the birth of a new sibling, death of a loved one, going into the care system) is often underestimated, the significance of the turbulent behaviour associated with adolescence is that it is experienced in one way or another by all individuals. A phenomenon occurs in which there is an accompanying and marked change in the way the school, the carer and the young person expect the adolescent to behave. What can be confusing for the young person is that, although his or her role may remain the same (e.g. sibling, pupil, 'child'), within that role different things are expected: the carers may expect more responsibility, the teacher may expect better performance, and both expect fewer errors of judgement. The young person may expect more independence. The teenage years can therefore seem like an emotional assault course for all concerned. The adolescent begins to develop views of his or her own that are not shared generally by adult society. There may also be conflict if the adolescent is assigned functions and duties for which they are not suited, and which they have not chosen (Guishard 1998).

Some foster carers choose to specialise in teenagers while others avoid them, simply because, in collaboration with the assessing agency, each carer carefully evaluates the type of placement they can provide. There are many reasons why carers prefer teenagers: the independence of the young person; the enjoyment of more mature conversation and activities; the opportunity to gain the specialist experience and skills acquired in working with teenagers; or simply because it balances the needs of the carer's own family.

In addition to the skills identified in Box 2.1, carers need to recognise that teenagers have their own joys and challenges, and that they have specific and important issues that they will have to accept and understand, such as the development of their identity and their sexuality; academic/exam stress; and significant peer group pressures. A foster carer who chooses to specialise in teenagers may already be particularly skilful at talking with and supporting children through whatever crises they may experience. Carers who specialise in teenagers will also need to be able to distinguish the 'growing pains' of adolescence from the raw expression of trauma that many children in the care system experience.

Specialist foster carers: treatment foster carers and contract/salaried foster carers

More experienced foster carers may wish to consider formalising their role by entering into a contract with their fostering agency to work with some of the most difficult youngsters (usually, but not always, teenagers). They will be paid an annual salary in addition to the allowance that they receive for the child. 'Treatment foster care' (TFC) is an idea from the Oregon Social Learning Center, and is a highly structured package of support to the placement, such as to provide intensive support to both the foster carer and the foster child. The Oregon model was aimed mainly at young people who were a high risk for committing crimes and with a history of breaking down successive foster placements. TFC has been well researched and is based on a theory of severe childhood trauma and the psychological disturbance that goes with that. The research has also extended to examining the day-to-day practice of caring for such children. Some fostering agencies may make a contract with a foster carer to take on the most challenging children, but without building in such a specific and prescriptive programme as the TFC model. The Government's recent proposals in relation to creating 'tiers' of foster carers, however, may in fact mean that all foster carers will have the opportunity to embark on a path that enables them to develop a main career as a foster carer (DfES 2006).

References

Bowlby, J. (1953) *Child Care and the Growth of Love.* London: Penguin.

Colton, M. and Williams, M. (1997) 'The nature of foster care: International trends.' *Adoption and Fostering 21*, 1, 44–49.

Corrick, H. (1996) 'The professionalisation of foster carers.' In A. Wheal (ed.) *The RHP Companion to Foster Care.* Dorset: Russell House Publishing.

Department for Education and Skills (DfES) (2006) *Care Matters: Transforming the Lives of Children and Young People in Care.* London: HMSO.

Guishard, J. (1998) 'The Parent Support Service: Brief family work in school.' *Educational Psychology in Practice 14*, 2, 135–139.

Robertson, J. and Robertson, J. (1969) *Young Children in Brief Separation.* John Concorde Film Council.

Ruegger, M. and Rayfield, L. (1999) 'The nature and dilemmas of fostering in the Nineties.' In A. Wheal (ed.) *The RHP Companion to Foster Care.* Dorset: Russell House Publishing.

Sellick, C. (1999) 'The international perspective of foster care.' In A. Wheal (ed.) *The RHP Companion to Foster Care.* Dorset: Russell House Publishing.

UNICEF (1997) *Children at Risk in Central and Eastern Europe: Perils and Promises.* Economies in Transition Studies Regional Monitoring Report No 4. Florence: UNICEF.

CHAPTER 3

Children in Need

Introduction

It is likely that for every reader approaching this chapter, the image of a 'child in need' will be different. Some will see a 'picture' – maybe like the posters or television advertisements produced by the NSPCC; for others a particular form of abuse or loss will be uppermost. So much can be said. This chapter aims to introduce some ideas and concepts that stimulate the reader's own thoughts, rather than attempt to say it all.

Throughout this chapter the terms 'child in need' and 'looked after child' are used. They are not interchangeable, but do often overlap: a child in need may not always be a looked after child, although a looked after child always has some status as a child in need. As a foster carer you will most likely be involved in providing a foster home in the short or longer term for children who are in need and who are also looked after, hence some emphasis is given to this term in the chapter. However, there are exceptions, of which disabled children are the most obvious example, and this will be discussed later.

The wood and the trees

Some time ago I [Suzanne McCall] asked a psychiatrist what his diagnosis was on a looked after child whom I had been **counselling** and who was giving many professionals cause for great concern. No doubt I was anticipating some fairly incomprehensible diagnosis that I would have to go and look up to understand, but after some initial thought he said, 'She's had too much of what she *doesn't* need, and not enough of what she *does* need.' Perhaps not the anticipated, neat, 'scientific' diagnosis but it summed up the basic issues quite plainly.

This seems such a good place to begin this chapter because it reminds us instantly of two important things that need some addressing from the start.

First, it reminds us of the basic things – the 'everydayness' of what children need in order to be given the best chance of growing up happy and healthy. Second, the psychiatrist's remarks imply some kind of balance sheet of needs and resources. The majority of children entering foster care will have a psychological balance sheet that we need to acknowledge. For many of them, the demands placed on them in undertaking the normal 'tasks' of growing up and of coping with what life has thus far presented to them has often far exceeded the resources available to them. The 'resources' are, of course, both social (who is there for them) and psychological (mental and emotional strengths and vulnerabilities).

The key, I suggest, to being most supportive to children in need is to be able to see both the 'tree' (the individual and unique child) and the 'wood' (the most commonly presented **psycho-social** profiles and needs of looked after children and children in need). Whenever we talk about children in need, we are separating them out as a group, almost – they have a special status. This is enshrined in the Children Act 1989. In Section 17 (10) of this Act a child is 'in need' if:

> S/he is unlikely to achieve or maintain, or have the opportunity TO SO DO, a reasonable standard of health or development with provision of services by a L.A.; or health or development likely to be significantly impaired,[1] or further impaired, without such services; or is disabled. (Smith 1991, p.8)

Of course, this special status is necessary and required; it is part of the process of shining a beam of resources on vulnerable and needy children. But it has a by-product, as most processes do: we can come close to regarding these children's needs as very different from other children's needs and almost, it seems, fail to keep in mind the most important of all the case 'facts' – that these are children. This may sound a little obvious (even a little disappointing) to readers who might be expecting cutting-edge insight from this chapter. However, it is my experience and firm belief that professionals become *least* helpful to children in need when they remember the really complex things (diagnosis, theoretical considerations, treatment plans, care plans, etc.) but fail to hold in mind the simple essence of what is staring them in the face: a child. This is most likely to happen when a child in need has diagnosed mental health problems. The foster carer is in the front line of this

---

1   **Significant harm** is a key term in the Children Act 1989 vocabulary. (See Glossary.)

scenario, since they are required to meet the simplest and most basic of all children's needs – feeding and bathing, holding and comforting (mentally and physically) – at the same time as negotiating professional systems (networks) that often deal in complex and sometimes conflicting theories and law.

It is important, then, to look a little at the 'wood' first – that is, to place the initial discussion of the child in need within the context of children in general.

The wood

Between 1940 and 1950, after gaining a PhD in **psychology**, Abraham Maslow developed what he called a 'hierarchy of needs' (Figure 3.1). His concept has been adopted and adapted by many differing theorists, and it is useful to include here because it is good, but straightforward, and it is still widely recognised as valid in the theories we work with about psychological health and ill-health.

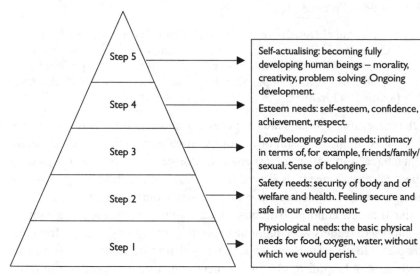

Step 5 — Self-actualising: becoming fully developing human beings – morality, creativity, problem solving. Ongoing development.

Step 4 — Esteem needs: self-esteem, confidence, achievement, respect.

Step 3 — Love/belonging/social needs: intimacy in terms of, for example, friends/family/sexual. Sense of belonging.

Step 2 — Safety needs: security of body and of welfare and health. Feeling secure and safe in our environment.

Step 1 — Physiological needs: the basic physical needs for food, oxygen, water, without which we would perish.

Figure 3.1: A representation of Maslow's 'hierarchy of needs', of which many different forms have been reproduced

Maslow intended us to think first about the bottom step of this ladder – the 'basic physical needs'. As with any ladder, to get to the top we must first negotiate the lower steps. Children in need will in general all have experienced disturbances in having their needs met on one or more steps of this ladder. In actual fact, of course, we all experience some disturbances of this kind – hence professionals talk about 'good enough' parenting: no parenting is perfect, and some failures might actually be important for the child to experience to build his or her own strengths. Notwithstanding this, for all of us there are some very basic needs that require meeting if we are going to be able to live each day, and to cope with – and truly meet – the demands of the future.

It is important that having these basic needs met helps protect us against the general 'ups and downs' of change in life – of what is termed 'psychosocial transitions'. These happen to us all: life's losses and traumas and the demands placed on us to adapt to new circumstances. Social workers, psychologists, psychiatrists and others often talk about the good care the child has received, and the resources available to him or her, as 'protective factors' (see Figure 3.2). Protective factors are those external and internal resources that limit our vulnerability to long-term psychological problems. Protective factors are linked to the term '**resilience**' (discussed in Chapter 6), but also to the concept (used extensively in this book) of the 'protective shield' of services that should surround vulnerable looked after children. One might also metaphorically describe the combination of protective factors and personal resilience as each person's own psychological 'protective shield'.

Each foster child you meet will have responded to losses in their lives in a different and unique way, depending upon a rather huge and complex combination of variables impinging on him or her – not to mention the variable that rather confounds all analysis, the 'person' or 'personality' of the child. (What every reader who is already a parent knows is that each one of their children has been 'different' from day one.) In the course of this book we will give you examples of these variables, but we can only touch the surface of a very deep pool of complexity. Real respect for the truly unfathomable qualities of human beings can have no substitute.

A special note is needed about children who fall into the 'in need' category as a result of being registered as disabled. The most common reason for providing these children with foster care is that they require **respite** care – sometimes this is short-term when the child's family undergoes some form of stress that leaves them temporarily unable to care for him or her, or there may be planned, longer-term or intermittent provision of extra care to families and children who have special needs. It would probably be true to say that there are sometimes different and particular issues raised in providing foster care in these circumstances, and this is covered more fully in Chapter 7. However, it should also be noted that the term 'disabled' may

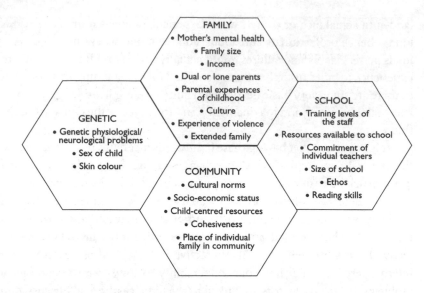

Example: in a family, the mother's mental health might be positively linked to a child's mental health if she is generally happy and secure, but negatively linked if she suffers from depression. However, factors must be considered in context – so, to go further, the mother's mental health may be a bigger risk factor if she is a lone parent, but only one factor that could affect the child's mental health if there is a large extended family that supports the mother and helps provide the child with security.

Figure 3.2: Interlinking systems / networks affecting the child's mental health: 'protective factors' and 'risk factors'. Many other variables could be included in each hexagon. Each factor will have an effect on the child, but how these effects show themselves, how powerful or weak their effect, will depend not only on the factor itself but the unique child and how the other factors combine.

sometimes be contentious and some families may feel unhappy that they have had to use this label in order to get the help and support they require.

The tree

Turning now to the individual child in need, the brief case study opposite may help the reader to re-focus. It cannot be presented as a typical scenario, although it has elements that are frequently part of the history of a child in need. In Chapter 6 the authors give more attention to individual mental health problems, so this is limited here.

'Food for thought': a brief case study illustrating Maslow's hierarchy of needs

In terms of Maslow's 'Step 1', Michelle receives all the 'basics' from her mother. As a baby she is fed, changed and clothed. However, her mother is very depressed, on benefits, and alone with three children. When her mother feeds Michelle, she puts her in a baby rocker and watches TV while she holds the bottle for her. At the earliest possible stage, she encourages Michelle to hold the bottle herself. Michelle's gaze is not met as she feeds, there is no talk, she is not held. Michelle's communications to mother that she has 'had enough' of her bottle and is full, or that she has pain due to wind, are not responded to until her crying becomes loud and desperate. Crucial opportunities to receive and understand intimacy are missed; just as crucially, Michelle does not learn about trust, control, **regulation** and pleasure. Michelle's growing experience of self may become distorted as she is left to cope with feelings that are overwhelming for her, and she has no verbal language to mediate and express these feelings. It is also unlikely that she will ever remember these experiences directly, or be able to verbalise them easily, since this capacity to recall directly is highly dependent on language, and many of these feelings are **preverbal**. She may, however, remember these experiences in other ways – in bodily experiences and distortions in her relations with food, mood, and other people.

At Maslow's Step 2 we find Michelle is never physically harmed or threatened, but she fails to feel safe: her earlier preverbal experiences of being uncontained emotionally and physically lead her to constantly feeling anxious. She therefore seeks out a good deal of reassurance from mother and others (she is hungry for attention and safety)…but somehow it is never enough. In any case, the more she demands from her mother, the further her mother retreats from these demands, as she cannot cope with her own feelings, let alone her toddler's. Michelle is also always hungry in other ways – she does not understand signals from her tummy that she is full, and she begins to become overweight. In addition to everything else, she begins to look unlovable, and others are not attracted to her physically or emotionally. New dynamics outside of the original ones with her mother begin to be set in motion – other adults and children show signs of rejecting her.

At Maslow's Step 3 we find problems are beginning to compound: Michelle's experience of self and others is that she is often rejected, her needs remain unmet, and she has not had 'giving' modelled for her either. She does not play well and has a low tolerance for frustration. By the time she is in infant school she is not seen as an unhappy child, but as an aggressive one.

At Maslow's Step 4 '**esteem** needs' are also largely thwarted. Emotionally Michelle is often at odds with others, but does not know why; the more she tries to demand attention and praise, the less it is forthcoming. She is also obese, and by the time of junior school this leads to further rejection by peers. She begins to be identified as a bully as she moves to senior school. When puberty hits, her experience of being further out of control of her body throws her into panic and anxiety. She blames all around her, but her real experience of herself is as someone who is disgusting and unlovable. Mother cannot help her, and she has not developed the good peer relationships that might have really helped her at this time. She begins to binge eat and then vomit, almost re-enacting her very early physical experiences of fullness and distress, emptiness and despair. She also becomes promiscuous: in an attempt to win over boys and be liked and included, she makes herself physically available to them. Less obviously (certainly to her, and especially to others), she is making the one bid she can for physical and emotional intimacy. When this comes to the attention of the school, she is referred to an assessment clinic that begins the process of trying to unravel her story and her meaning. The clinic becomes increasingly concerned by her mother's failure to attend appointments and Michelle's poor physical well-being and mental health. She is also refusing to go to school. Her mother eventually feels she cannot cope with her daughter's outrageous behaviour and demands, and Michelle is accommodated by the local authority.

No-one has been able to piece together her story, as Michelle herself is very loath to trust anyone and tends not to be able to express her feelings verbally. There is little history when she arrives in your care. There is much concern from professionals that she may have been sexually abused and that this may have led to her eating disorder and her sexual activity.

What can be made of Michelle's story? Certainly, what should be highlighted is that this example could have contained an infinite number of different outcomes: none of this is written in stone. The comments above about complexities are echoed here: the most wonderful capacity of human beings' flexibility, such that the same experience will be interpreted and lived with uniquely by different individuals. We can say for sure that the answer to the question 'What does 2 + 2 equal?' will be 4: no complexities here. We cannot say the same for people: people are not like simple maths. If you like, the question then becomes 'What equals 4?' The answers to that question are infinite.

For a significant number of children coming into fostering, there has been sustained failure in meeting a number of their basic needs. Michelle probably fits this scenario. What you might wish to consider about Michelle is how one single factor or variation in her history (given the complex inter-connection of variables we discussed above) might have changed the outcome, not only of her being accommodated, but of how she learnt to think, feel and experience herself and others. For example, the presence of a warm, attentive aunt who helped Michelle to learn that she is worthy of care and love might have altered her **internalising** (see Chapter 4) of herself as unloveable: at the very least, Michelle might have had alternative experi-ences to draw from, and this could have provided her with more tools with which to approach others and build relationships that could have sustained her emotionally, or added resilience.

For some children there has been a catastrophic failure of needs being met and huge losses encountered – as in severe trauma and abuse – and many refugee children will fall into this category. Very often when we consider children in need and mental health problems, these are the children that come first to mind and get the most media attention. Trauma, and the defini-tion of what constitutes trauma, is not fixed, nor is it separable from other aspects of someone's life. Severe trauma can interfere with a person's ability to process thoughts and emotions, and post-traumatic stress disorder (PTSD) has attracted much attention as needing quite specific treatments. Traumatic experiences, and the processing of these in terms of mental health, will be addressed in Chapter 6.

A jigsaw can be used as an analogy to think about the different forms of loss a child can encounter that may lead to mental health problems. (Remember that analogies are useful but imperfect ways of describing such ideas.) If you are doing a jigsaw (for example, of a famous face) it is quite possible for there to be several bits missing from the picture from the begin-ning, but still you can identify who the famous person is when the jigsaw is complete. I think of this analogy as being close to the harm that Michelle encountered in terms of her own identity. So many needs went unmet (or were only partially met) that her sense of identity – her sense of herself – was fragmented. Clearly, the more jigsaw pieces are missing, the patchier becomes the picture, and at some point so many key pieces are missing and the jigsaw is so incomplete that the face is unrecognisable. With a more catastrophic failure, or severe abuse, sometimes a whole section of the jigsaw is missing, so that the 'picture' has a gaping hole in it. In this case one might think of a young person who has been so severely abused that they never experienced certain key stages in Maslow's hierarchy at all. Psychologically and emotionally, they may not have the basic resources to process much of what happens in their lives at all.

Before ending this section on the individual child, I'd like to mention three things about the case study of Michelle. The first of these concerns Maslow's highest step of 'self-actualising needs'. It is important, when encountering children in need, to aim to understand how it is that they are trying to *survive*. For me, Maslow's idea of 'self-actualising needs' connects with a perspective in psychology that says everybody is trying in the best way they can to survive in the environment in which they find themselves: they are trying to **'actualise'**. This is broadly defined as the 'humanistic' approach in psychological therapies. Very often when a child in your care is driving you to distraction, it is natural to find yourself tuning in to the negatives – how they disrupt, how they hurt themselves, how unhelpful certain ways of behaving are, and even how their behaviour does not make sense to you. Tuning into these behaviours as part of a very necessary survival strategy can be helpful in refocusing for yourself, and also helpful in redefining the young person's behaviour for themselves.

Second is what we can call 'everybody's story'. When we talk about 'mental health/psychological needs' our thoughts are focused on the *minds* of others. Michelle's story describes how her *body* also experienced and subsequently held part of her story. As a counsellor, I have learned to pay attention more and more to the *physical* presence of the client: how they look, talk, walk, sit, dress, and the mannerisms that make up who they are. Our bodies hold vital clues to every aspect of our being, and this is most certainly the case with children in need. Very often they have huge issues about self-care and this manifests itself vividly in their relationship to their own bodies. If you look at the body, and bodily 'way-of-being', of yourself or someone you know well, you can become more **attuned** to the messages held there.

Last, the trap of 'X = Y' equations: we all look for causes and reasons why things have happened, it is part of being human and striving to anticipate and predict what will come next. I think of it as an essentially very human characteristic. However, it is also a very fallible process, and in your capacity as a foster carer you need to be wary of interpreting what is seen, and attributing causes to it. Michelle presented some aspects of behaviour many young people do when they have experienced **sexual abuse**.

- She engaged in sexual relationships in an attempt to form relationships very early and she engaged in many of these indiscriminately.

- She had problems with eating normally and regulating body-size; in fact, she became bulimic.

- She seems not to be able to verbalise her feelings (which may give the impression that she is hiding something).

- She has poor attachment patterns.

In making presumptions that sexual abuse would be the story that she would eventually tell when she felt safe enough, not only would professionals be leading her to tell this story, but also ignoring much that did not fit into this picture. It is a very delicate area of the work to be done with young people: to be able to see and respond to patterns that can be thought of as warning signs, while still allowing for the individual meaning and story to unfold – to be aware of the wood, but able to appreciate the tree.

Taking care of your own needs

There is also the category of foster carers in need, alongside the children in need. Consistent, reliable support is vital for all foster carers. Many find support patchy at best – yes, it is there when things go *really* wrong, but many do not get enough dedicated, professional, regular support as a right. There are a number of models that are used by local authorities – mentoring, buddying, groups, link workers…usually a combination of these. However, the feedback the authors have received is that more consistent help is needed for many dealing with challenging children. If you are to be able to help contain a child in your care who is struggling, you can also allow yourself to feel **contained** by others who will help you to deal with your own feelings of anger, confusion and anxiety. They can also help you to feel great about the joys that come along, and this is very important for you to mark, both for the child and for yourself. Perhaps, then, the 'protective shield' for looked after children, of which foster carers are a major part (see Figure 2.1 on p.22),

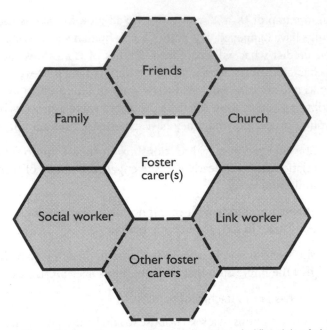

The foster carer(s) can add more elements to their own 'protective shield' until they feel they are supported. Suggestions have been made above about what some of these elements may be, but they can be re-designed to suit the individual carer.

Figure 3.3: The foster carer's protective shield. Foster carer(s) need to consider the elements of their own 'protective shield' so that they can enhance their ability to consistently care for the child, and for themselves, and for others who may be dependent upon them.

could also be considered in the context of your own needs. Let us 'zoom in' to one section of the shield – that is, the foster carer – and ask what it is that enables him or her to provide a high-quality caring environment (Figure 3.3).

At the end of this chapter is a list of questions that may be useful to think about when seeking help. Foster carers may find it difficult to access the kind of help that they need (Maguire 2005). The questions here provide the reader with a basic checklist for thinking about who can help them most in the professional system, and about what might be useful when seeking consultation and accepting help.

What I would like to suggest also, as part of your own reflection on this chapter, is that you take some time out to think about your own childhood. Each person reading this book will have unique experiences of being a child and of being parented. In some way, shape or form – directly or indirectly – these memories will, more than any theory, influence how you foster and what you want out of fostering for yourself and for the children. Where are your wounds? Understanding some of the elements in your own balance sheet (strengths, vulnerabilities, blind spots, etc.) can only help you to understand better and deal more effectively with the tough times, be they moments, or week after week of struggling with a very distressed child who is pushing you to your limits. Perhaps you can allow yourself to remember what were the very best of times for you when you were young, memories that might still evoke a 'feel-good' sense in you. Perhaps, also, you can remember times when you felt most unhappy, and why this was. I think this kind of exercise is best done with another person whom you trust, but this doesn't have to be a therapist!

Last words

Having read this chapter, it may be that some readers feel a little cheated. Where were all the 'facts'? Facts can be great comforters when you are trying to figure out anything, let alone struggling to foster a child when you are confused and distressed and don't know what to do next. I have often found myself leafing through books, trying to find answers for counselling young people I am struggling with, and, I must admit, my library is now rather vast! Perhaps we can say that asking questions and exploring possibilities is a crucial process, but the answers may not exist in the ways we have often been taught to think of them.

Donald Winnicott (a figure who, like Freud, made significant contributions to understanding the mind) coined the term 'good-enough mothering'. By this he meant that the child doesn't need a *perfect* parent. In the context of a book on fostering, perhaps we can rewrite this as 'good-enough parenting'. It seems important to think about how this chapter may, or may not, have moved you further on in your thinking about what 'good-enough parenting' might mean for the child in need in your care. If you have been left with confusion and uncertainties that spring to mind, then it would be good to note these down right now, before moving on in your reading.

Hope for new levels of awareness, if not always answers.

If you turn off the light in a room at night, at first you can barely see. You bump into things, trip up and lose sight of where you are. If, however, you wait a while, you find that slowly, bit by bit, more and more can be seen as your eyes adjust to the new circumstances. Your other senses, too, become more valuable: hearing, smell, touch and 'intuition' – senses you may be used to forgetting to use.

Working with troubled young people is often a bit like that too. It requires a huge amount of patience to wait to see what can be seen, and trust a new, more **instinctual** focus.

Basic checklist for getting help with a fostered child

You might find this checklist helpful in focusing on what is needed if you are talking to others about a child in your care who you may be struggling with, or just trying to move forward with. Other questions may come to your mind as equally important, and it would be good to note them down to make this list more useful to you.

Before the consultation you might like to think about the following

- Why am I concerned?

- What behaviours am I noticing in the child, and what feelings am I noticing in myself?

- Who should I contact? (Social worker? Link worker? Anyone else?)

- Who can help me, in this situation, with this child, at this time, MOST?

- What do I want out of this conversation with this professional?

- What will make a difference? (Do I have just ONE thing, or a list?)

- When do I want help – how urgent is this? Are there longer-term goals?

- How will I best be able to use the information I am given – for example, will a phone call do, or do I need to meet the professional, or have something written down as well?

After the consultation

- Did I feel able to say what I wanted to say…and if not, why not, and what needs to be done about this?

- Did I feel that my points were understood and listened to?

- How will I know if I was listened to – did I agree future feedback/action plan/meeting?

- Are there any 'timetables' that were agreed? If not, why not, and should there have been?

- Do I feel the call/meeting made a difference? If so, was it to me, or the child, or both?

- Would I do anything different next time?

References

Maguire, S. (2005) 'Mental health literacy and attitudes in foster carers: Identification of factors that influence help-seeking.' Unpublished dissertation supervised by J. Guishard-Pine. University of East Anglia.

Smith, F. (1991) *Personal Guide to the Children Act 1989*. In consultation with Professor Tina Lyon. Surrey: Children Act Enterprises.

CHAPTER 4

Relationships

Introduction to the idea of relationships

Psychology tries to understand both the relationships and dynamics between people (external) and the relationship people have to themselves – or their 'idea' of themselves (internal). This chapter aims to introduce some concepts around the topic of relationships and, in the first section, to extend the usual, rather fixed, concepts about what a relationship is. As a foster carer, you may feel ideally that you have a lot of 'information' about a child prior to their coming to live with you. Even when you get the information, it will not tell you all of what you need to know or understand about this young person, baby or child, and how they will impact on your own life and the life of your family. Training can help prepare for certain eventualities, but the rest of the learning is made *in relation* to the children themselves, as you become **attuned** to them and they to you. Each child will change you, and change aspects of your relationships with others, and vice versa.

Making the decision to foster will have involved thinking carefully about the well-being of any other children in your home, and you may feel that you wish to protect them from some changes, or even some influences. The assessment of your suitability to become a foster carer will have included talking with other members of your family (if they are in the household) regarding how each member feels about fostering. However, at the early stages of assessment it can be hard to think about the extent and manner of change and challenge that the entire foster family will encounter.

What is also often less considered is that the child you foster comes with family ties, and increasingly the agreements around contact between the looked after child and his or her birth family – siblings, parents, grandparents – will involve the foster family. Fostering 'a child' might be a misleading image; current legislation demands that the child retains a relationship with the birth family, school and community (unless there are very strong reasons to do otherwise). In every sense, the child walks into your home, not just as an individual, but as a 'system' of prior and present relationships, externally and internally. With older foster children this can mean a long and varied history of family and previous foster placements. Also relevant to the idea of relationships is that recent research (Sinclair *et al.* 2005) indicates that a child will benefit from help to think through the complex emotions of 'fitting in' to a foster family while still retaining strong family ties, with or without there being a possibility of returning home. The emotional pull of the idea of 'going home' while in foster care needs to be given space within the foster family if the child is not to feel very stressed with ideas of blame, guilt, betrayal, and so on.

Representations and relationships

Before jumping in at the deep end of this chapter, it seems important to mention one significant psychological idea that underpins much of the theory around human relationships and the theories that have been developed to account both for healthy relationships between a parent or caregiver and child, and for not-so-healthy relationships. This underlying idea, quite simply put, is that from day one (as infants) humans create internal (within the mind) **representations** of external things. The 'things' can be a person – such as mother – or slightly more abstract, such as the relationship between one person and another. Intuitively, of course, the reader already knows this in the most obvious of senses, since you can usually recall an image of someone like your mother or father pretty well instantly. But you can also recall much more complex representations, such as how two people relate, how you feel about someone past or present, or even future. For example, one can imagine anticipating the birth and care of a baby, based on all sorts of representations about past experience, or transferred experience from observing others' reactions to birth and parenthood, and so on.

In other words, we create internal 'worlds'. These internal worlds vary in how accurately they represent what is thought of as external 'reality'. In Chapter 3 we referred to the need for us all to respond to change, and described change as '**psycho-social** transitions'. How well our internal world can adapt to keep up with external 'reality' is very relevant to mental health and psychological well-being.

We are all, always, relating in some way to something, someone, some idea, belief or value – *and* relating to ourselves. In this sense we are always located in multiple 'external' systems – families, organisations, social groups – and at the same time relating to multiple 'internal' systems – that is, representations of these external systems. This idea is echoed throughout this chapter in various ways, and throughout the book (for example, in the 'protective shield' concept). You may appreciate, then, how such common statements as 'I have no relationship with him/her' are nonsensical, since the phrase holds complex ideas about what 'having' a relationship might mean (such that we can say that we 'do not' have one). 'Not having' a relationship is, in a sense, also a way of 'having' a relationship – but a relationship perceived in the negative sense. No matter how hard we try, it would seem that we can never get out of relating to others in some way.

Case study: Mary and Maggy

Mary has an internal representation of families, based on her own experience of a very happy childhood where she was loved and cared for by two caring parents. She sees parenting as something which she really looks forward to when she 'grows up', as her parents seem to have enjoyed bringing up her and her brother. Relationships seem fairly 'easy' to her, since she sees that they can be made and sustained. As a result of her experiences, Mary also has a good internal representation of herself: she is clearly lovable, since she can see that others have loved her. She does not often doubt that she can be happy in the future. Mary is likely to view the world as a place in which she makes her own way towards what she wants.

Maggy has a very different representation: her idea of a family is based on something that can abruptly change and cannot be trusted, as she has had various stepfathers and her mother 'disappears' from time to time. She sees people being hit and shouted at a lot, and she and her sister have never got on because they have had to compete for affection. To Maggy, families mean uncertainty, arguing and hurting a lot of the time. She does not recognise herself as being of any real value – her relationship with herself has been damaged – since she has not felt loved. Maggy may feel that the world is not a place in which she gets what she wants or needs, and that life is more about coping with what gets thrown at you than determining for yourself some of your own fate.

Note: Neither of these 'examples' leads to a fixed outcome: however, we can imagine that Maggy might have some difficulties being in intimate relationships.

When thinking about fostering, it is important to think carefully about your own representations of concepts such as 'family', 'care', 'love', etc. What can be predicted is that the children you foster will often have different (sometimes very different) representations of these concepts. This can lead to very different expectations, and conflict if not recognised early. A very present theme in research undertaken by Sinclair *et al.* (2005) was what a foster 'family' really meant to children being looked after. There were many views represented from the children they undertook the research with, but issues around fitting in and sameness and difference were important. (Chapter 5 explores these themes in terms of invisibility and visibility.) Children looked after may be very adept at picking out instances of where they feel less loved or accepted than the foster carers' 'other' children. But also there were very real barriers to feeling normal in even very settled placements: both children and foster carers became very resentful of the limitations and rules around developing 'normal' relationships (such as police clearances required before a foster child could have a sleepover with a friend), and this also potentially affected the foster carers' relationships. For example, if a looked after child had previously been sexually abused, then foster carers felt that having their friends/family to stay in the home (as would any 'average' family) was subject to rules that made it difficult on many levels. When fostering it may be hard to preserve your own representations of what family means.

Today's media explosion has also fundamentally widened any discussion that can be had about relationships. Adolescents are a case in point, since they face an enormously complex and intrusive barrage of 'proxy' relationships of every sort, every day, through TV, magazines, radio, etc. In soaps on TV, for example, adolescents pick up so many adult and peer figures to model on, and it is very usual to hear them describe what kind of relationship they think they have with each character. These things are a given; it is not possible to do anything other than mildly control adolescents' access to the media if you feel it is unhelpful (and even if you stop a young person watching TV, they will get a lot of images via peers), and therefore it would be better if we could work *with* such a powerful force: to make it, as much as possible, a therapeutic friend instead of a foe. For example, if a young person is prepared to sit with you and discuss how they feel about a character in *EastEnders*, then right away this is vital relationship-building which can be therapeutic (for example, you listen to them, can join with them in the discussion, and can talk about your own opinions while respecting what they say), and also they are giving you a wealth of information about how they see themselves, relationships, and the world, if you can just hear the messages. They might say, 'I really hate so and so in *EastEnders* because...'

Here you have the beginnings of a discussion that can have meaning both in terms of the detail of what they hate, or like, and why, but also in terms of your developing relationship. When I am **counselling** young people I am always aware of opportunities for therapeutically using what they choose to talk about, rather than trying to get them to talk about what I think needs discussing.

While there are certainly some continuities, the complex relationships we have to all around us are also constantly changing and evolving if we have a healthy self-esteem: they are not useful to us as 'fixed' ideas. For example, in the course of reading this book, your own relationship along one dynamic will probably shift and change and evolve significantly. You may change from feeling that you do not 'belong' to the profession of foster care…to feeling that you have more of a relationship with the idea of being a foster carer…and indeed…become part of the profession and form many relationships to other foster carers and professionals based on an evolving sense of your own identity.

Many children in need have had severe disruptions to their relationships with others, and to their relationship with the idea of themselves, and these two are linked in a complex way. One theory about this particular set of issues is called 'attachment theory', and below is a description of some parts of this theory.

Why attachment theory?

Why, out of all the theories on relationships between parents or caregivers and children, does attachment theory present as one of the most important to describe here?

If, at a very basic level, we can say that attachment theory addresses how we think about ourselves and our relationships with others, then at this very simple level we are all aware of how important these basics are to mental health: it is hard to be 'well adjusted' if one dislikes oneself and feels uneasy with others. Attachment theory is also an accepted and much used theory throughout the professions and agencies you are likely to encounter in child care. This does not mean that you must think the same way, but it can be useful to understand how others make professional judgements. Attachment theory will be, in some shape or form, at the root of judgements made about the child's relationships with parents and at the root of possible future pre-dictions about the child's ability to form different relationships. It may inform decisions about whether a young infant or child should come into care, what contact will be established between child and parent or caregiver, whether a child could return home, or be looked after permanently, or be a very obvious candidate for adoption. Attachment theory also has a place in the arena of mental health diagnosis and treatment. It is said that attachment theory is also a very useful theory to professionals because it can be applied in a test: social workers in particular will be aware of the 'strange situation test' developed as a way of measuring the quality of relationships between children and a parent or caregiver and making some assessments about what kind of attachment the child has to that person.

Attachment theory (see Figure 4.1) was developed by John Bowlby in the 1940s and claimed that human beings have a biologically based (**instinctual**) attachment 'system' that is activated whenever there is an external or internal threat (perceived threat). Bowlby claimed that 'maternal attachment is as essential for healthy psychological development as vitamins and proteins are for physical health' (Flanagan 2005, p.40). Although not exactly the same, Bowlby saw the **instinct** to attach a little like other instincts a baby would be born with – like the instinct to feed. The very young child has very few of its own resources to help it eliminate the threat

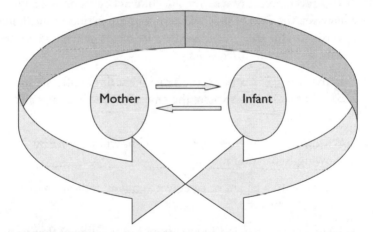

Bowlby said that the mother and child are participants in a mutually self-regulating, interacting system. (That is to say that the actions of one affect the actions of the other, and that this then affects the next interaction – and so on.) The child has its own, very basic instinct towards attachment that serves as a survival mechanism, and this is activated after birth in relation to one figure. The mother also has an attachment system that may be regarded as an adapted form of her own, younger, learned attachment (i.e. what remains with the adult of what she has learned from her attachment experiences as a child). The two become involved in a mutually regulating system that attunes to the child's needs and adapts and reacts to change intuitively. Other figures, such as a father, may become very important figures as secondary attachments, but there is only one primary figure.

Figure 4.1: A representation of Bowlby's view of the mother and infant attachment system

by itself and so we see what is termed 'attachment behaviour' being triggered frequently: the infant looks to a perceived familiar figure with whom he or she has built a specific attachment to eliminate any sense of threat. As the infant begins to attach (or attempt to attach) to the parent or caregiver, learning that takes place in the earliest stages of the relationship between the infant and the parent and/or caregiver (i.e. **preverbal** and **non-conscious**) has a powerful and long-lasting effect on the child's interactions with others and with him- or herself (self identity). Bowlby's theories are still current today, but many others have moved his work on and extended the research and application. Bowlby did not state that the relationship with attachment figure was the *only* relationship to take place, but that it was an important and specific one that was key in the process of full emotional and psychological development.

Seven key points for understanding attachment theory are as follows.

1.   Infants are 'programmed' (from birth or before) to seek proximity to an 'attachment figure'.

2.   The development of a secure attachment occurs principally between the ages of 0–12 months, but the period of maximum sensitivity for attachment needs to be met is generally between four months and three years.

3.   In the absence of a threat the attachment figure offers a secure base from which to explore the environment physically and emotionally.

4.   When parted from the figure, the infant will respond by showing 'separation protest'.

5.   'Clinging' to a parent or caregiver is not an indication of a secure attachment.

6.   The reciprocal relationship between the attachment figure and the infant will be 'remembered' (although not consciously) as an internal working model, and will form the basis of future assumptions.

7.   The 'attachment dynamic' (i.e. the form of relationship) does not end in infancy. Although it is often present in a **latent** way, it can be triggered at times of stress – for example, if an adult is in a difficult marital situation.

(Adapted from Holmes 1994 and Adcock, White and Hollows 1991)

In a positive environment, where one could say that a child securely attaches to a primary caregiver, the child is thought to learn about itself as worthy, as 'OK', as loveable – he or she develops these ideas about him- or herself because of the positive mirror image of themselves that is reflected back to them by the primary caregiver. The child also learns and develops better since this basic security allows them to explore as they grow. Secure attachment is also thought to help the individual to learn about being human: because the child learns from the mother about being attuned (sensitive to the other, able to be **empathic**), the child can go on to develop this capacity in other relationships. (You might also consider how this fits in with Maslow's ideas of the hierarchy of need, discussed in Chapter 3.)

When attachment is not secure it is generally described as 'insecure'. About 60 per cent of attachment is secure (Carr 2002). Insecure attachments can be categorised in a variety of ways, but the most basic and perhaps useful in this context is 'inhibited' (associated with abuse and **neglect** or punitive parenting, with the child frequently displaying difficulties in dealing with changes, withdrawal and aggression, possibly extreme watchfulness) and 'disinhibited' (associated with institutional or multi-placement settings where young children may be excessively clinging, but show little selective attachment as they become older – almost 'over-friendly').

Whether or not a child in your care is believed to have a disorder of attachment (an insecure attachment of some kind that affects their ability to form stable relationships), or this is ever discussed in these explicit terms, it seems reasonable to assume that many foster children may experience issues with attachment to some degree. In almost all circumstances one can see that the experience of coming into foster care, even for very small babies, will normally elicit attachment behaviour as it has been defined: failure for this behaviour to be elicited would possibly be cause for concern. For example, if a child in your care is separated from a parent and seems not to mind, what could this indicate about what they have learned and internalised about relationships?

The issue of blame is frequently raised, directly or indirectly, in issues of attachment. It is important to bear in mind that a child may have difficulties in attaching for a number of reasons, not all of them which might be ascribed to the capacities of parents/caregivers. Amongst the other reasons for difficulties in attaching might be a childhood illness, which may involve experiences of sustained pain in early infanthood. Also, children with neurological differences, such as those who have developmental disorders such as autism, could be expected to show differences in attaching. Autism (see Chapter 7) by no means blocks a child's capacities to attach, although clearly those at the more severe end of the autistic spectrum will suffer more problems. The majority of autistic children will show a preference for a caregiver, and are able to benefit (largely speaking) from attachment in the same way as all children are thought to, in terms of social, emotional and **cognitive** skills.

Applying attachment further: 'how', not 'who'

> The idea that attachment fulfils the instinctual needs of a human baby (beyond feeding) is an important concept of attachment theory. It directs us to understand the mother–infant relationship as one that affects all humans, thus encompassing all cultural boundaries, and/or ethnic child rearing practices. (Reebye *et al.* 1999, p.8)

Attachment theory has been criticised because it seems to say that mothers (i.e. women) are essential to look after the infant, and because it seems to be based on a very western view of family – especially the concept of the nuclear family. Understanding whether attachment theory holds some truth beyond a very western view of the 'ideal' family unit started early in the theory and there has been a continuing debate since. Reebye *et al.* have done much work collecting results of studies done on attachment across cultures, and conclude that the theory seems to hold some global truth about the first relationships.

Without a doubt, the '**standardised tests**' referred to earlier as being important in measuring attachment need careful rethinking and adjustment to be culturally sensitive. For example, Reebye *et al.* found that it was important to understand that cultural practices might affect the degree to which the child would explore the environment, and that therefore researchers could not rate a child as 'insecurely attached' just because they seemed slow in moving away from a parent and/or caregiver, or they might welcome an adult parent and/or caregiver very differently. This seems like common sense, but so often in the past, common sense has been lacking in understanding cultural differences. In reviewing research, Reebye *et al.* also found that studies looking at the issue of 'multiple mother figures' in parts of Nigerian culture have found that 'children formed attachment relationships with many maternal figures, but they demonstrated a preference for one relationship over all others. The preferred maternal figure was the one who held them most frequently and had more opportunities to interact with the child' (Reebye *et al.* 1999, p.10). However, they also reviewed research undertaken by Sagi *et al.* (1985) regarding kibbutz children in Israel, and they note that these studies have consistently shown more *insecurely* attached children among those who also sleep communally at night, compared with those who returned to parents at night. This seems an interesting finding.

The role of men as attachment figures has also been more widely discussed. For example, Nicholson (1984) describes how psychologists studying the interactions between mothers and fathers and infants have been able to understand more fully that the father need not just be the 'secondary' figure in an infant's world, but may bring very different, but very important, interactions into play. Nicholson also notes that good contact with the father significantly helps an infant to socialise later in life. However, Nicholson also notes that 'children seem to seek different things from their parents: security from their mother, friendship and stimulation from their father' (1984, p.132). In a dual parenting situation it would appear that parents make different contributions to the child's development. In a lone-parent situation there is no reason why the primary attachment figure could not be male. Attachment is not based on *who* the individual carer is in this respect, but on *how* they are *in relation* to the infant.

The idea of 'culture' reminds us that all theory has to be understood in context. The history of many therapies, like psychotherapy, has been a journey of widening out the understanding of the individual in context in many ways, and today most therapies have some idea of the '**systemic**' approach: that is, that an individual must be understood in relation to many systems that have complex effects on them, as described earlier in this chapter. We can see how these 'systemic' ideas have grown throughout time by looking just at this theory of attachment. Figure 4.2 represents a very simplified version of how the psychology of infants has been primarily understood over the last century, and shows how our understanding of psychological development has consistently taken on more and more of the infant's environment.

There is growing research in the field of **neuroscience** to suggest that the patterns of early relationships, like attachment, don't just affect us but *shape our brains* in the process. In *Why Love Matters – How Affection Shapes a Baby's Brain* Sue Gerhardt (2004) describes a perspective that is growing in strength. Simply stated, it claims that the newborn infant is what she terms an 'external foetus', and, as in any foetus, the physiological/chemical systems are still being formed. In particular, while the baby does come equipped with its own tendencies, the brain is in such an early stage of organisation that the very shape of the brain's **neural pathways** are formed in response to early relating and attachment. Brain scanning technology is

1. The infant alone – understanding human psychology and behaviour primarily through understanding the internal psychological dynamics (pre-Bowlby).

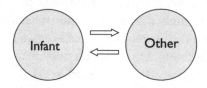

2. The infant in relation – understanding human psychology and behaviour in relation to another.

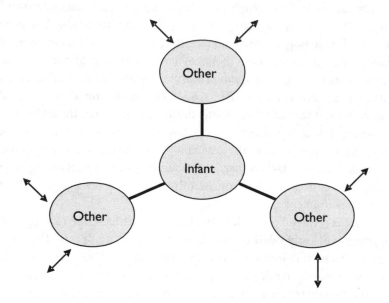

3. The infant in relation to a whole system – the infant responds to, and changes, a whole system of relationships around itself. Each person in the infant's system has been influenced by other systems, and so potentially the diagram has endless connections.

It is interesting to note how the expanded idea, over time, of how to understand a child's psychology and development (as represented above) has been reflected in the 1989 Children Act, which now places a high importance on appreciating the WHOLE system of the child's contacts when deciding on a placement.

Figure 4.2: The 'external foetus'

doing much to support the idea that we learn how to be human from our neural pathways upwards. Gerhardt says:

> The most frequent behaviours of the parental figures, both mother and father, will be etched in the baby's neural pathways as guides to relating. These repeated experiences turn into learning, and in terms of the pathways involved in emotion, this consists primarily of learning what to expect from others in close relationships… Our basic psychological organisation is learnt from our generalised experiences in the earliest months and years. (Gerhardt 2004, p.211)

Attachment, relationships and fostering the child: ways forward

Given what has been said about children with attachment problems, given that as a foster carer you will be receiving into your care a child who has had at least one experience of a relationship separation (when they come to you), and given, too, that there has been much research into attachment issues, it would be reasonable to expect that someone, somewhere has found solutions, or good pointers, for caring for children with such issues.

Attachment theorists are inclined to the view that the foundation stones laid down in early childhood about how to build attachments and sustain healthy relationships to other human beings tend to be difficult to change. In terms of foster care providing **reparative** (healing) or even corrective relationships with children whose attachment patterns have been very disrupted, the news, therefore, is not all rosy according to the theory and the recent neuroscientific findings. Sinclair *et al.* put this suggestion another way from their research findings on looked after children (including foster care). They say:

> A problem facing children in all settings is that their personal difficulties do transfer. Thus there is a high correlation between children's childlike attachment scores in one setting and their scores in another. By contrast the benign effects of good parenting in one foster care setting do not necessarily transfer to another. (Sinclair *et al.* 2005, p.256)

Put simply, this seems to say that 'good' learning in a positive foster placement is often not obviously manifest in the next placement. This seems important for carers to appreciate in understanding young people's behaviour when they come to them, and in considering the expectations that they have of how the young person will behave.

Treatment foster care

Some reading this book will already be familiar with a new (to Britain) model of fostering called 'treatment foster care' (TFC), from the Oregon Social Learning Center, which aims to provide structured interventions for children who are at a high risk of foster placements breaking down – either because the level of psychological damage at a very early stage is already very evident in a young child, or because an older child has clearly been unable to survive in foster placements and there have been a number of placement breakdowns. These children are often very challenging to foster. TFC is based on wide-ranging research into both the theory of childhood trauma and attachment problems, and the outcome of years of research into the kind of day-to-day *practice* of caring for such children that seems to make a difference. In the following summary they succinctly capture the essence of the issues:

1.   Children who have received inadequate care or who have been exposed to high levels of prenatal and early life stress *do not respond typically* to the efforts of caregivers to nurture and support them.

2.   [It is] important to acknowledge that current behaviours of these children were often adaptive to the early environment.

3.   Nevertheless, without support, it is difficult for foster parents to override interactional processes (rejection, betrayal) that lead to relationships failure, etc.

4.   Conversely, with appropriate support, the therapeutic potential of relationships can be activated.

(Slides reproduced by permission of Philip Fisher, presenter of the Treatment Foster Care training programme 2005; Fisher and Hyoun 2007)

If relationships are at the source of a good deal of emotional pain, then they are also at the root of emotional well-being – they can hurt, and they can heal. In (1) above, Oregon note that children may not always be able to access the care that they may be given in foster care, and they pose the question, 'If love is not enough, then what is?' Point (2) echoes the findings of Sinclair *et al.* – that children who arrive in foster care may already be locked into ways of understanding, experiencing and processing relationships that are very difficult to change; in fact, one could say that, since close relationships have been associated with troubling, difficult feelings for the children in their past, when foster carers offer a caring, loving relationship this can be extremely threatening for some very damaged children and actually trigger a stress response (i.e. a reaction exactly opposite to the desired one).

It is a dilemma, and the Treatment Foster Care programme, and other projects, have developed a series of techniques for fostering such children which can be helpful to think about. It is worth remembering, however, that this is a very challenging and difficult area of work in fostering, and help from agencies such as children and families mental health clinics will usually be sought to support the child and the foster family. To put these issues in perspective, Sellick (1996, in Adams, Dominelli and Payne 2002, p.282) notes that '65 per cent of all children in local authority public care for one year were fostered. Most of the children spent very short periods in care, that is, less than 14 days for 50 per cent of the children.' *It should be remembered, then, that what has been presented in this chapter represents the most challenging edge of fostering children with significant issues in the longer term.*

Common themes and suggestions

The following summarises some current ideas on managing children with attachment issues. Many new views about caring for children who have attachment issues can be linked directly to the ideas in this chapter, but caution should always be exercised in applying any one technique to any one child without sound knowledge and advice.

Structure

Children with attachment problems need firm, age-appropriate structure. The idea of structure is relevant to all areas of care – from daily routine, to structured hugs and structured play. The central concept is consistency of care, and of reliable outcomes – that is, 'This happens then, this happens there – if I do this, then that happens, etc.' It is thought that, because of their early experiences, these children will not have had such consistency and therefore can feel unsafe (unboundaried). They have been left to decide too much in the past for themselves. Freedom can only be appreciated once one feels safe in having it.

Discipline

Again, discipline needs to be age-appropriate, but the idea of very *predictable* rewards and consequences is emphasised *for all ages, including adolescents.* (Nancy Thomas (1997) notes that the word 'punishment' is really unhelpful with children who have attachment disorders. Punishment is what they may try to elicit from you, but consequences that are predictable, fair and consistent is what the adult carer must deliver.) Oregon provides an extensive model for such monitoring and this includes a model for adolescents. Also highlighted is the need to be clear in giving reasons for rewards and consequences, but not over-explaining: move on after a consequence is given, rather than engage in any negative discussions with the child or young person.

Supervision

Young people with emotional and/or behavioural issues need extensive adult supervision. Certainly initially (for the first month or so), Oregon believes that a young person should be allowed *no* unsupervised time with peers, but that this can be earned later in the reward system. However, they also note that, in order for positive changes in behaviour to be sustained, the amount of unsupervised time must be limited in the longer term.

Nurture

The idea that the adult must take responsibility for emotional and physical nurturing in a structured way is seen mostly, as one would expect, in relation to younger children. However, it is certainly not exclusive to them. The most radical of programmes for children with severe attachment problems suggest that a child should not get a hug when they ask for it, but must be *given* hugs by the adult throughout the day. For older children, while physical contact can still be important, nurture can be shown in many ways, but noticing and reinforcing the good things a young person does is key. Within the idea of nurture also is the idea of eye contact. We know that this is vital for babies, but it is suggested that older children may benefit from foster carers making a *focused use of expressive, kind eye contact* every day. While this may be very useful, some caution needs to be exercised in understanding the meaning of such eye contact for the child, because of the culturally sensitive nature of eye contact.

Effective and 'different' help for foster carers, parents and young people

Each person in the system often needs a professional who will 'take their side' rather than trying to understand and work with everybody's needs. Clearly, this is most often needed with those looked after children who have the more challenging behaviours.

Understanding

This may seem painfully obvious as a requirement of any foster carer for a child who comes into their care, but given that children with attachment difficulties can be very hard to relate to, they are often not only 'difficult to handle' but hard to like and hard to understand. You may feel as if you are continually flinging yourself against a wall. Reminding yourself to 'touch base' with your knowledge and understanding during very stressful times can be a good way of getting needed 'time out' for adults, to help them contain the child.

'Honeymoons'

Nancy Thomas (1997) reminds carers to expect (or at least prepare for) a 'honeymoon period' when a child comes to them with attachment issues. All the authors have witnessed such a pattern in placements: the child arrives, seems to settle fine, the behaviours are not as challenging as were anticipated, and everyone begins to relax, then, seemingly from nowhere, things begin to go wrong. Nancy encourages professionals to translate 'moving' a child as 'traumatising' a child. This new term prompts us more often into remembering how difficult it is for them. If a child comes to you and apparently settles in rather effortlessly, what does this say about their past experiences?

The no blame position

Foster carers are most likely to be successful in handling difficult behaviour if they are inclined not to take behaviour as personal to them – for example, to understand that a distressed child may consistently reject the *idea* of you (i.e. any foster carer figure), rather than you *personally*. This echoes ideas earlier in the chapter that attachment issues 'transfer' from placement to placement, rather than necessarily being specific to the individual carers.

This is only a limited selection of ideas that seem reasonably accepted in the literature. Some of the current advice seems to be the opposite of what we might intuitively do with children who have already suffered so much (relax rules, give and take a lot, loosen boundaries). The balance of nurture and structure is important to get right; however, the underlying principle is always to allocate the emphasis on control of relationships back to an adult, who then leads the infant/child through (or sometimes back through) the basic steps of relationship building and emotional **regulation**.

Conclusion

The message from this chapter should certainly not be that we are all nothing but the product of our previous relationships and that very little can be done to change this. (You will recall the research findings on kibbutz children, which may demonstrate that children can be very resilient to a number of changes if even just one basic factor is consistent.) Neither, however, can it be true to say that our previous relationship experiences do not have a powerful effect on us. At the end of this chapter is a short list of questions designed to help you reflect on your own experiences and to think about those of the children who may come to you. It is not inclusive, and there will be many areas that you can develop yourself.

Offering a home to children with attachment issues can leave you feeling de-skilled – this is a frequent reaction. It is not possible to mend all children that come your way, but it is important that you are able to hold some hope for them, especially when, faced with loss and confusion and feelings of inevitability, they cannot hold it for themselves. Sometimes holding some hope means really appreciating and noticing even the smallest changes or seemingly mundane things that are OK about the child's time with you, rather than expecting huge change and major breakthroughs. And part of the theme of relationships in this chapter, but also more widespread in the book, is the message to reflect on what relationships you can develop with others (partner, family, friends, professionals, community, etc.) to help you care for the child and give them a sense of belonging too.

Questions to consider

- What patterns of attachment do you think you notice in yourself? For example, is there anything that you remember distinctly from your own childhood and feel strongly about now?

- Are you aware of any other adults whose attachment patterns you think are still very noticeable? (For example, your partner.)

- How do you think love is best shown, and how do you think you know that someone *cares* for you? Is this the same thing as someone loving you?

- How about hate?

- Do you ever confuse the two – love and hate?

- Who is easiest in your family to get to know if you are a 'stranger'?

- Who is hardest to get to know?

- Where could a new foster child find real physical space in your home, and what emotional spaces do you think there are for them to grow to become an important part of the household?

- How flexible do you think you and your family can be to change yourselves in response to a new foster child, rather than the other way around?

- How will you discover what the idea of love and hate feels like to the foster child?

- How vulnerable would you feel if you had to pack your bags now and move in with another family who are probably unknown to you? What would *you* like done to give you room to grow?

- And finally: what strategies would you use to get this new family to accept you – and how does your thinking this last question through help you understand the strategies that others use?

References

Adams, R., Dominelli, L. and Payne, M. (eds) (2002) *Social Work· Themes, Issues and Critical Debates.* Hampshire: Palgrave.

Adcock, M., White, R. and Hollows, A. (eds) (1991) *Significant Harm.* Croydon: Significant Publications.

Carr, A. (2002) *The Handbook of Child and Adolescent Clinical Psychology: A Contextual Approach.* Hove: Brunner-Routledge.

Fearnley, S. and Howe, D. (1999) 'Disorders of attachment and attachment therapy.' *Adoption and Fostering 23,* 2, 19–30.

Fisher, P.A. and Hyoun, K. (2007) 'Intervention effects on foster preschoolers' attachment-related behaviours from a randomized trial.' *Prevention Science,* in press.

Flanagan, C. (ed.) (2005) *Applying Psychology to Early Child Development.* London: Hodder & Stoughton.

Gerhardt, S. (2004) *Why Love Matters – How Affection Shapes a Baby's Brain.* Hove: Brunner-Routledge.

Holmes, J. (1994) 'Attachment theory – a secure theoretical base for counselling?' *Psychodynamic Counselling 1,* 1, 65–78.

Nicholson, J. (1984) *Men and Women: How Different are They?* Oxford: Oxford University Press.

Reebye, P.N., Ross S.E., Jamieson, K. and Clark, J. (1999) 'A literature review of child–parent/caregiver attachment theory and cross-cultural practices influencing attachment.' From *Sharing Attachment Patterns across Cultures: Learning from Immigrants and Refugees.* Toronto, CA: St Joseph's Women's Health Centre, Parkdale Parents Primary Prevention Project. Retrieved 13 May 2005 at www.attachmentacrosscultures.org/research/index.html

Sagi, A., Lamb, M.E., Lewkowicz, K.S., Shoham, R., Dvir, R. and Estes, D. (1985) 'Security of infant–mother, –father and –metapelet attachments among kibbutz-reared Israeli children.' *Monographs of the Society for Research in Child Development*, 50 (1–2), 257–275.

Sinclair, I., Baker, C., Wilson, K. and Gibbs, I. (2005) *Foster Children – Where They Go and How They Get On.* London: Jessica Kingsley Publishers.

Thomas, N. (1997) *When Love is Not Enough: A Guide to Parenting Children with RAD – Reactive Attachment Disorder.* Glenwood Springs, CO: Families by Design.

Training resource
Fisher, P. (2004) 'Effective treatments for youth and children in foster and adoptive care.' Paper presented at Parents for Children Conference, London, 28 September 2004.

CHAPTER 5

Visibility and Invisibility

Introduction

'**Visibility** and invisibility' in the title relates to what can be seen of a person, such as skin colour and dress; it also relates to the attitudes, family traditions and beliefs that are expressed and made visible through a young person's behaviour. Looked after children who join a new family will experience both similarities and differences between their way of life and that of their new carers. Some experiences will magnify their sense of visibility and some experiences will leave them, or facets of their identity, invisible and without **validation**.

This chapter takes the notion of a young person's visibility or invisibility and shows how the experience affects their developing identity.

Joining a new family

Most people have an intuitive sense of what family means to them. Yet if we assume that each family is unique and then consider the diverse make-up of families in the UK – the nuclear family, extended family, single parents, step-families, unmarried parents and so on – and add to that the differences that attitudes bring to family life and family structures, attitudes that are informed by faith, racial or cultural identity, social class and so forth, then one can begin to appreciate the elastic band of family forms mentioned later in this book.

Looked after children come from all sections of society – although children from poorer and minority communities in the UK are known to be over-represented within the care system, and to remain in care longer. Differences between a looked after child's foster family and their family of origin can present the young person with significant challenges. As mentioned above, differences and similarities between birth and foster families can lead the young person to experience a feeling of visibility or invisibility.

> ### Case study
>
> A young South Asian looked after child holding her black foster carer's hand in the supermarket presents a visible difference within the child's community. The visibility and the difference appear to the child to be reflected back to her through the gaze of her onlookers.
>
> At home, when the same child refuses to speak to, appreciate or engage at all with the man in the house, this puts a strain on the couple's relationship. The child's lack of engagement leads the male foster carer to believe he is failing to support his partner or get through to the young child – but the young child learnt with her mother that men don't see her and will take her mother away and leave her abandoned. The child is aware of the strain that shows in the female foster carer and doesn't understand why she gets so angry with her – the child's mother wasn't like this.

As in the case study above, visibility can lead to feelings of being misunderstood and then **marginalised**. However, in different circumstances visibility can also lead to positive effects and feelings of validation. Invisibility, or not being seen, can either lead to the feeling of being marginalised, or it can have the effect of being led to feel normal and so **validated**. Again, it is dependent on the set of circumstances, or context.

> ### Case study
>
> A mixed race looked after child is in the supermarket with his foster family, who have the same skin colour and hair as he does. The community response to the looked after child supports his wish to be accepted as 'normal' in a normal family.

The scenario above shows how a looked after child, who, in his community, is not distinguishable from his foster carers' own children, experiences a validating effect as a result of his invisibility.

Through case studies and exercises this chapter explores the subject of visibility and invisibility and the consequent experiences of validation or

marginalisation for looked after children. It shows how these issues affect the development of a looked after child's growing sense of identity, what foster carers can do to help, and what the impact may be on the foster carer.

Identity and looked after children

There are many thoughts and models that aim to make sense of how a person (young or old) develops an identity. Generally, western twentieth-century ideas of identity raise the importance of the influence of the mind, biology, society, or spirit (the transcendent) – or of a combination of some of these factors.

Identity, character, personality and personhood are brought together here and generalised in the term 'identity'.

Sigmund Freud (1856–1939) pioneered the hugely influential ideas of **psychoanalysis** (Kovel 1991). Freud proposed that a person develops, biologically, through childhood to maturation and adulthood. This maturation is influenced by how the child is parented and **socialised**. However, through childhood, forces within the child's mind, including infantile sexuality and the effects of trauma, build a catalogue of neurosis and trauma. This catalogue survives into adulthood, but remains barely hidden in the unconscious mind of the adult – hidden in each of us and hidden *from* each of us. The neurosis and trauma are then triggered by life events to impact on us, influencing our behaviour and **perceptions**, and leading us to experience irrational fears or phobias and repeat unwanted patterns of behaviour.

The psychoanalytic approach proposes that what minimises the development of these forces within the mind is unhindered play through childhood and the protection of the child by its parents, family and adult carers.

Carl Gustav Jung's (1875–1961) theory of **analytic psychology** (Kovel 1991; Read *et al.* 1978) developed from his work with Freud. Jung's ideas differed from Freud's significantly in his theory of the mind. Analytic psychology proposes that the forces within a person's mind (Freud describes infantile sexuality as just one of these) go far beyond the experience of any one person but arise from the deepest history of human existence. Analytic psychology proposes that a person's **subconscious** is shaped by mythic themes (archetypes) such as 'the Great Mother' or 'the Hero'. Jung connects the notion of identity and personhood to mythical and spiritual, **transpersonal** heights. It is this transpersonal element that is triggered and impacts on our everyday living, but again, it exists under the surface of our socialised identity.

Thomas (1999) proposes the idea of 'identification by proxy', or a false identity that presents an acceptable or 'I'm fine!' persona to those perceived as not trustworthy. Thomas applies this idea in particular to young people who suffer stereotyping and learn to expect discrimination. Consider a looked after child who is 'fine' but shy with his peers and with his teacher, and whose post-abuse symptoms leave him feeling, inside, highly suspicious of people all of the time.

Thomas's idea implies the existence of an authentic but hidden identity waiting to come out when it's safe. Some ideas about identity suggest a fixed, core identity that will always remain 'whole' but may be rendered unreachable by layers of fear, confusion or uncertainty within the young person's view of the world and their own acceptability in it. **Humanism** is a philosophy that extends this view. Carl Rogers developed the **Rogerian** idea (Kovel 1991) that we each have at our core a kind of animal or free nature that knows how to **thrive**, a 'whole' person. However, the events and expectations of living have put our true natures into a kind of sleep. The process of awakening involves making honest contact with our selves through emotions and sensuality, rather than intellect.

Whereas the ideas summarised briefly above each have a logic and coherence of their own, the **existential** point of view deliberately dismisses any idea of structure. Existential thinkers say we have made up the structures, models and ideas to reassure ourselves: we tell ourselves that, if we know the structure, we can be in control of life and have nothing to fear. Existentialists say life is chaotic, uncertain and basically godless. As for identity, existentialists say we are simply incomplete people in the world – we are each always growing and changing into who we are becoming. For existentialists, although this may be scary, it is not a pronouncement of doom but a key that opens the lock to real living.

Systemic theory and systemic (or family) therapists look to the way families in particular, but also events, communities and culture, shape and influence the behaviours, beliefs and moral obligations of the individual, and how that individual in turn shapes and influences the people and events they encounter.

This idea that identity may be constructed through social interaction ('**social construction**' through social processes) turns our attention to the effect that relationships, communication and groups of people have on a person. Accordingly, an individual's identity can be seen as continually developing in response to their 'web' of relationships, time, place and culture.

Models are perhaps most usefully thought of as tools rather than one or another being the 'truth' – giving the true description of identity, for example. Instead one tool may be really handy, where another just isn't right for the job. This chapter makes reference to ideas of social construction as it helps to take into account the particular life experiences of looked after children: transition, trauma, life history, the foster family's way of life, visibility and invisibility.

Regardless of the model, what we hold on to is the idea that you cannot understand an event unless you take into account the situation the event arises in – the activities, the thoughts and the types of relationship. So a slap on the back will hold one meaning in the course of play, another in a greeting, and yet another meaning if it is undesired.

Take a look at the case study over the page. If Carmen's panic attack could be understood in the context of her being justifiably frightened, the school might feel better able to support her – a prepared safe place to go to where her emotions can be accepted would make a difference. A learning mentor who is qualified in **counselling** could be allocated to offer Carmen some help to let go of the terrible blame she attributes to herself. The mentor could also keep school staff and residential home staff in touch with Carmen's needs.

Without the context, or background knowledge, the behaviour could not be understood.

A looked after child's way of living will be significantly shaped by the values and lifestyle of their birth family, their peer group, religious beliefs, their experience of the care system, past abuse or abandonment, or other significant contexts at any one time.

So a struggle between a carer and a ten-year-old child over the household's bedtime routine could be influenced by the child's feeling of unfairness because her peers can stay up for much longer. Or perhaps the child needs to be in charge, something she learnt in her family of origin. Perhaps for some looked after children the routine signals the end of safe family life and the possibility of more abuse. The teeth-brushing and wash routine is a horrid chore for many children – what if it simply didn't happen before, and the skills weren't developed? Has someone called her dirty before? Perhaps hiding or pretending is the habitual resource for coping with this experience of shame and not fitting in?

Differences of this kind can appear to be unfathomable, cause friction and rub up against what a foster carer has been brought up to believe is everyday and normal. A way towards understanding the lives of looked after children is, then, to remain aware of one's own assumptions about what is

Case study: Carmen

Carmen had been quiet all weekend, but that was not unlike her. She lived in a children's home and often didn't feel like talking after contact with her father, which took place on Fridays after school.

Monday, first thing, she had mathematics. She enjoyed maths and her residential key worker told Carmen that that would cheer her up.

Carmen had a panic attack in the maths lesson. She thought her heart would explode, so she curled up into a ball, held her hands to her ears and yelled 'No!' over and over again to block out the sound of blood rushing. Carmen's teacher was frightened and thought Carmen was too severely mentally ill. 'This is too much for our school! This is her third mainstream school; perhaps she would be safer in a psychiatric unit?'

Like the teacher, Carmen was also frightened. She was frightened that her father couldn't cope with seeing her any more – wasn't that why her mother left them? [Her mother was in fact in prison.] Carmen was frightened of the other children in the residential home, she thought that they would reject and bully her if they knew that she could make her mother and father abandon her. Carmen kept herself quiet, but she was sure the other children would work her out soon. Carmen was frightened that, if she was moved from the residential unit, she would have to move schools again too.

Carmen only ever felt safe when distracted by maths.

She decided to talk to her maths teacher but, as she thought of calling out, her feelings overwhelmed her and her heart beat faster. Now even Carmen's own body is scaring her.

right, even through the most unremarkable routines. As mentioned in other chapters, the foster carers' energy is much better spent on getting to *know* the child, rather than trying to 'get through' to the child.

So, a young person's sense of who they are is intimately linked with their relationships. Differences and similarities between the young person and those who are their significant relationships, including their foster carers, affect this development of their sense of self.

Young people from minority communities and communities who traditionally face discrimination have a challenge to find a positive sense of who they are in relation to the majority culture.

Invisible differences of minority communities, such as the gay and lesbian community, then further affect how a gay or lesbian looked after child relates to others, and how they compare and judge themselves against others. Invalidation that arises as a consequence of invisibility can prepare the ground for shame and poor self-judgements and the kind of marginalisation mentioned earlier. This will then be exacerbated by their experience of homophobia.

The invalidation of the gay or lesbian looked after child will influence how that young person values their own experience, and so stunt or repress the growth of their identity, or even generate a self-hatred of their identity. What foster carers can do – heterosexual foster carers in particular – is similar in pattern to what foster carers in transracial placements can do to support the healthy identity development of their fostered children. This is expanded below.

Black and Asian children in the UK, with support from their families and communities – whose awareness of racism influences their parenting – can build **resilience** and grow up knowing their skin colour does not make them ugly or worth less than their white friends. Children growing up in households that share, enjoy and love their cultural identity develop resilience to deal with the acts, words and the expectation of discrimination in other places, the neighbourhood, the playground and on television, that might otherwise significantly undermine the development of a positive sense of their own self-identity. Invisibility or the absence of images that represent one's cultural identity similarly impacts on an individual's ability to develop a positive self-identity.

The family's support of the child – its knowledge and living of its cultural heritage, and connection to a robust community – builds resilience in the child with regard to racism. Foster carers of transracial placements have a responsibility to address the potentially damaging effects of their visible difference. Learning about racism and the looked after child's cultural heritage is an ongoing process – keep learning. Connect to relevant community groups through community-focused newspapers, radio stations and magazines, playgroups, barbers and salons, parent groups. Listen to the wishes of the child, but don't mistake ambivalence on the part of the looked after child for disinterest; you may need to be assertive.

Heterosexual foster carers of gay and lesbian looked after children have a similar challenge. Learn about homophobia, keep learning. Groups for gay and lesbian young people exist across the country. Groups for parents of gay and lesbian young people are also widespread. If there isn't one in your area, why not start one? *Gaytimes* magazine is available in most newsagents across the UK. The *Pink Paper* is available online. Both publications will list contact details for these and other groups.

Mixed ability urban schools across the UK commonly adopt a convention of mixing classes, even classroom tables, by gender, ability and **ethnicity**, and yet the playgrounds of those same schools become largely inhabited by uniform ethnic groups. Young people will seek validation through cultural sameness in their friendship groups.

Take a few minutes now to remember a time when you felt as though you couldn't fit in, or you felt misunderstood. Perhaps someone was angry with you and you couldn't understand why, or vice versa. Perhaps you can recollect having to be 'normal' at work, on a day that was a very sad day for your family? Perhaps it was a time you felt you were not given a fair chance to be understood, or getting so lost in a new town that you just wanted to go home. These events may have demanded a great deal of emotional effort from you, maybe they left you tired and drained.

How did you move on, or recover from these feelings? It may be that how you move on from experiences like this is so natural to you that it is hard to see, but do give it some thought. Perhaps you simply got home, or talked to friends, listened to 'your' music, ate chips; perhaps you needed to seethe for a while first, before having a good moan to a colleague; or maybe you just stopped and gave yourself a moment?

These 'everyday' experiences of marginalisation can be of use in reminding us of how we learn to manage such discomfort.

The significance of family home life, culture and peer group culture to the development of a young person's growing identity is an important consideration, in understanding looked after children, for the network of professionals (**corporate parent**) who support them, including foster carers. The challenge here is to acknowledge and attend to the inevitable disruption that is a consequence of displacement for the young person's identity formation and their own sense of who they are within their new environment.

Case study: Triston and Keith

Triston, 6, and Keith, 5, are brothers who were born in a rural parish in Barbados. The boys arrived in Britain with their mother soon after Keith's third birthday. They settled in London. Although they did not join an extended family there, they became active members of, and were actively supported by, the local Seventh Day Adventist Church community, a community that exceeded 1500 regular churchgoers.

Following a psychotic breakdown and a number of relapses, the boys' mother was admitted to hospital and the boys were taken into local authority care. They were placed with a black couple, Simon and Andrea Clarence, who were both born in Britain to Jamaican parents. Simon and Andrea had no children of their own. They too were active members of a church community and travelled weekly to a Jehovah's Witness Kingdom Hall. Both foster carers described themselves as working evangelists.

Four months following the boys' initial placement, Andrea shared her concerns and frustration during a placement review with the boys' social worker. Andrea described Triston as being overly watchful of her and withdrawn most of the time, at times refusing to speak for whole days. She said his watchfulness of her was 'getting under my skin!'.

Keith, in contrast, was 'uncontrollable and undisciplined'. Although his behaviour was not so bad with Simon, neither carer could risk taking him on their house calls – as was routine for evangelists – as he had repeatedly run screaming through the homes they called on. Simon had grown very fond of the boys but, like Andrea, feared that they might have inherited their mother's illness and needed treatment, and perhaps even placement in a specialist therapeutic setting.

The boys' social worker was particularly saddened to hear this, as he had pictured the boys with the Clarences and knew they would appear to anyone as a 'normal' family. He was also pleased to place the boys with a couple who could focus on them and raise them as Christians, understanding the importance of Christianity to their birth mother.

Over time and with the contributions of a play therapist and life story work, a different picture of the boys' culture emerged, with consequences for the boys' transition needs at that time.

Through storymaking with play figures, both boys demonstrated a shared perception of a 'mother' figure as someone who they could curl up next to, where they would be silent, warm and fed.

Father figures did not appear to inhabit their play worlds. However, the traditional attributes of the authoritarian and nurturing father appeared to be shared by the vast numbers of smiling adults who would inhabit their play worlds.

This led the therapist and social worker to wonder about the meaning of Keith's screaming in the context of rural life and Barbados's open spaces, where screaming would be acceptable as play. And then the support of a large Adventist church community, who would be happily accepted by the boys as authoritarian 'father' figures. Perhaps there is a cultural difference between that of the children and that of the Clarences' church and 'work' community, where such behaviour wouldn't fit in? Perhaps Keith was calling on the strangers to recognise his screaming as play, but nevertheless to respond with active attention to him and effective boundary-setting.

Triston became more able to talk; he said he wanted to curl up with his mum. He talked about being breast-fed…then said immediately after that 'Auntie Andrea doesn't stop talking'. Perhaps Triston had interpreted his mother's silence as a signal that he could receive the comfort he needed.

Foster families, too, face the challenge of attending to the effect on their own family life of the new addition to their household or family.

As mentioned above, the first challenge for foster carers with regard to the identity formation of looked after children is to acknowledge the disruption that is an inevitable consequence of displacement. Removing children and young people from the web of relationships that make up their communities, from the cultural environments that are influencing them, and being influenced by them, with all of the hopes, expectations, beliefs, obligations, roles and duties that evolve through those relationships, will leave many children confused as to how to behave, and then how to cope within their confusion. Or it may compel the young people to work hard to recreate the web that they know they can fit into – even if it was a web defined by a culture of abuse.

Chapters 8 and 11 present accounts of the widespread appreciation, in children's services and in government legislation, for the importance of supporting looked after children within their communities.

Foster carers take the very special place in a looked after child's life, as the adults who welcome them into their world and accept them for who they are. Simple as this sounds, the process can nevertheless be profoundly intricate and demanding. Welcoming a child into your world, however, is not something for a foster carer to feel is their responsibility in isolation; it requires the support of their community, the child's community, and a community of professionals.

References

Kovel, J. (1991) *A Complete Guide to Therapy, from Psychoanalysis to Behaviour Modification.* New York: Pantheon Books. Hassocks, UK: Harvester Press. Reprinted by the Penguin Group.

Read, H., Fordham, M., Gerhard A. and McGuire, W. (1978) *The Spirit in Man, Art and Literature.* Princeton, NJ: Princeton University Press.

Thomas, L.K. (1999) 'Communicating with a Black Child: Overcoming Obstacles of Difference.' In P. Milner and B. Carolin (eds) *Time to Listen to Children: Personal and Professional Communication.* London: Routledge.

CHAPTER 6

Psychological Issues for Looked After Children

Mental Health

What is child mental health?

Mental health unites the physical and emotional well-being of a child. This means that the child develops the skill to connect the impact of their bodily functions with the recognition and expression of feelings – in themselves and in others. It is evidenced by a child's ability to be creative and also to find the emotional energy to survive negative life events – especially those that lead to feelings of loss, such as looked after children may experience through loss of, for example, birth family, school, healthy body (as in the case of children experiencing **physical abuse** and failure to **thrive**), friends, community, hope, trust…etc. This ability is sometimes called **resilience**.

Children who are mentally healthy will usually have developed a sense of right and wrong. They will also have the self-discipline to accept the consequences of their misbehaviour. One could say, therefore, that social and moral development are also linked to mental health. In his classic book *Childhood and Adolescence*, J.A. Hadfield (1987) referred to these ideas in his account of his study of children resident in children's homes. He did not feel that it was appropriate to describe and discuss children's psychological issues just from observing 'abnormal' behaviour. He concluded that it was crucial for psychologists also to observe 'normal' behaviour in order to understand children's psychological development. From his research, Hadfield observed that children needed a balance of boundaries, routines and freedom if they were to be well adjusted. He introduced the important concept of mental 'hygiene'. Mental hygiene is the maintenance of mental health and the prevention of mental and emotional disorders.

Young Minds is a specialist organisation that promotes and provides information on the mental health of children and young people, and also supports carers. Young Minds has been helpful in attempting to widen the definition of child mental health. Mental health in children is a multi-dimensional process of growth and change made up of emotional, intellectual, psychological and spiritual components. A child's motivation to develop and maintain wholesome relationships is also relevant to their mental health, as is their capacity to learn from the full range of positive and negative personal experiences, and to use these as an opportunity to increase their self-understanding and knowledge of others.

All children and young people have to deal with a range of factors which put their mental health at risk, as part of their day-to-day living. Some are better equipped to cope with life stresses (despite inner city deprivation) because of the effectiveness of their 'protective shield' (see Chapter 2). It is important that we build resilience in our children and young people from as early an age as possible, enabling them better to deal with the natural stresses of life, such as **psycho-social** transitions (see Chapter 4).

Research done by the Office for National Statistics (ONS) and the Institute of Psychiatry at the Maudsley Hospital and reported by Young Minds has shown that between 10 and 20 per cent of children and young people have a mental health problem, and a smaller percentage will have a severe mental illness. Children who live in inner-city areas and children in the lower socio-economic classes are more likely to be diagnosed with a mental health disorder. People from minority ethnic groups are more vulnerable to stress because of racism and the higher levels of poverty and unemployment in minority ethnic families. However, although they have relatively high levels of diagnosed mental health problems in adulthood, they are not more likely than white children to have a mental health problem.

What is the difference between a mental health problem and a mental health disorder?

'Mental health problem' is an umbrella term for mental health disorders but can also be used to describe emotional problems that may be more short-lived than disorders. One could argue, for example, that it is entirely 'normal' for children to show fear, worry, shyness or stress at different stages of childhood and in response to different life experiences, e.g. feeling depressed after a bereavement.

Mental health disorders, however, are chronic (i.e. have been part of the person's life for several months) and have a significant effect on the person's ability to enjoy a fulfilling life. Mental health disorders are also specifically defined by psychiatric categories on instruments such as the *Diagnostic and Statistical Manual on Mental Health Disorders (Fourth Edition) (DSM-IV)* which is based on definitions made by the American Psychiatric Association, or the more widely used *International Statistical Classification of Disease and Related Health Problems, 10th Revision (ICD-10)*, which is based on definitions made by experts within the World Health Organisation (WHO). Examples of mental health disorders are:

- *emotional disorders* – e.g. phobias, anxiety states and depression; these may also manifest themselves in physical symptoms

- *conduct disorders* – e.g. stealing, fire-setting and antisocial behaviour

- *hyperkinetic disorders* – e.g. significantly high level of activity or low level of attention

- *eating disorders* – e.g. pre-school eating problems, anorexia nervosa and bulimia nervosa

- *pervasive developmental disorders* – e.g. delay in acquiring a skill such as speech; may affect primarily one area or pervade a number of areas, for example in autism

- *habit disorders* – e.g. tics, sleep problems, enuresis/encopresis

- *post-traumatic syndromes* – e.g. post-traumatic stress disorder (PTSD)

- *somatic disorders* – e.g. chronic fatigue syndrome (CFS), enduring headaches, unexplained digestive problems

- *psychotic disorders* – e.g. schizophrenia, bipolar (manic-depressive) disorder, drug-induced psychoses.

(Source: NHS Health Advisory Service 1995)

Stress and distress in children

Adults often do not remember what creates stress and anxiety in children. We are all essentially the same (on a spiritual level), but basically *different* (on a physical level). Yet, when dealing with children, adults often refer back to their own experience as a child, or that of their own children. Sometimes foster carers have their own history of **neglect** as a child, and they have an overwhelming need to 'right' things for the looked after child, for themselves, and indirectly for their own parents. The fact is that child (a) *is* different from child (b), and both are most certainly likely to be different from the foster carer as a child. It is therefore better to try to understand the actual foster child's distress. Ask the child not 'How can I get through to you?' but rather 'How can you get through to me?' Identifying with a child's pain is crucially to know, in its truest sense, what it is to be a human. Think about how the piercing cry of a baby worries adults – we recognise how we might be feeling if we were to let out such a shrill cry.

We are now going to look at the psychological impact of the stress and distress of physical abuse, **sexual abuse** and domestic violence, **emotional abuse**, neglect, and living with mentally-ill parents and drug-abusing and substance-misusing parents. We will also introduce you to other traumas (such as bereavement) and present some ideas, not only about what you can do to help, but where you can get help for your foster child when their needs exceed what you and your support network can cope with. The information on these areas is adapted from the Royal College of Psychiatrists 'Mental Health and Growing Up' series and Young Minds websites, and Herbert (1987). The website addresses are given at the end of the chapter.

The psychological effects of child abuse

The importance of addressing mental health concerns around child abuse cannot be overstated, because the psychological impact of it is likely to go on to affect the child's behaviour, thoughts and feelings as an adult. Child abuse occurs across all ages, races, religions, and socio-economic backgrounds. Although girls are three times more likely to endure sexual abuse, boys also experience it. The reasons why some adults choose to abuse a child is not clear, but there is some evidence to show that some parents may harm their children if they themselves were brought up in an abusing family and did not have the opportunity to come to terms with the fury or grief that they felt about what had happened to them. Other parents may harm their child if they abuse drugs or alcohol, or if they are mentally ill themselves. In fact, many substance-misusing parents have also experienced abuse in their childhood or adult life. The agreement is, however, that there are many parents who cannot cope with the stresses of the task of parenting, or with the stresses of living, and abusing their children is a symptom of this.

Sexual abuse

Sexualised behaviour is part of normal development. Children will show some interest in eroticism from playing 'kiss chase' in the infant school playground, to looking and giggling at photographs of naked breasts or men's genitals in the secondary-school playground. There are some types of sexualised behaviour amongst children that, although considered 'normal', can feel abusive to another child, particularly one who have been abused by adults at a younger age – for example, touching another child's bottom or looking up a girl's skirt. Sexual abuse that leads children into foster care is not the kind of introduction to sexual activity that most of us would have experienced, nor of the kind mentioned in these examples. Sexual abuse usually involves an adult in a position of power over a child, but it can involve two children. The abuser can be male or female, though it is usually a male. He or she can be a stranger, but is usually a family member or close family friend. Sexually abusive behaviour can range from touching 'private' parts of the body with clothes on, or exposure to pornography, to full, penetrative rape.

Living in a violent home

Many other children suffer abuse by living in a violent home. In families where there is domestic violence, children witness the violence through all of their senses. They may begin to associate smells and tastes with a particularly vicious beating that they witnessed with their eyes or ears, or both, because of the memory of a smell or flavour at the time of the beating. Domestic violence affects one in four adult women and one in six adult men, and some children in these homes are also abused. When children witness violence, they learn that violence is a very powerful method for getting your own way, or for humiliating another person. This experience can be carried into the school setting and sometimes to the foster care situation. More important is that they learn that they can hurt people who are close to them, only to make it up with them afterwards, as though violence is of no consequence. Witnessing violence teaches children that there are no limits – morally or physically – to how you treat someone that you 'love'. With strong and sensitive foster care, however, they can learn to distinguish between what their feelings tell them they want to do, and the moral judgement that they must make in choosing whether or not to act on those feelings. The foster carer can also teach them how to alter those feelings, so that they do not enact the damage that they feel they really would like to do (anger management).

Neglect and emotional abuse

In child care practice, 'neglect' relates to depriving the child of the experiences that actively promote their physical and emotional well-being, such a good standards of nutrition, hygiene, and activities to support and promote their physical development; opportunities to explore their environment so that they can develop problem-solving and other intellectual skills; opportunities to hear conversation and to use language in a range of contexts (e.g. with children of a range of ages, and with adults outside of the family; in instructional and structured contexts, as well as unstructured settings such as play in the garden, park or playground); and opportunities to develop their senses so that they can gain increasingly refined skills in discriminating between and labelling and memorising shapes and objects, sound, texture, tastes and smells – which also aids their development of concepts. Children who have been subjected to prolonged periods where they are deprived of an environment that promotes healthy development have been neglected. Neglect has far-reaching implications for their rate of growth, physically and intellectually. Table 6.1 (on p.77) identifies some of the main consequences of child abuse and neglect.

Neglect can be wilful or, increasingly in modern times, it can be due to the ineffective parenting of substance-misusing parents. It can also come about as a result of a genuine lack of knowledge and experience of nurturing and wholesome parenting. All forms of abuse include emotional abuse and neglect at some level. However, a child who is wilfully abused emotionally by their parent will have experience of a parent who places little value on having a mutually fulfilling relationship with their child, and shows this by being indifferent to their needs, or actively behaving in such a way to make the child feel worthless, unwanted and unloved. The child who is emotionally abused will tend to have low self-esteem. Low self-esteem is characteristic of a child whose life is unbalanced with a lot of negativity and gloom, whereas a child with high self-esteem will tend to have good academic achievement, be an active, expressive, emotionally intelligent, sociable, confident person who can appropriately adapt their role to meet a given situation.

Growing up with a substance-abusing or physically or mentally ill parent

Physical and mental illnesses in adulthood is common. Many children will have some contact with a parent or other family member who has periods of poor physical or mental health. Children with a substance-misusing parent, or a physically or mentally ill parent, will often have to spend periods where they have no access to their parent on an emotional level. If a parent is admitted to a psychiatric hospital or to rehabilitation, the child may lose both physical and psychological contact with their parent.

Children who have grown up in such an environment can appear to be over-compliant. They will often attribute their parent's state to whether or not they do as they are told. They may have said to themselves 'If I am good then Mummy/Daddy won't take any more drugs' or 'the cancer won't come back'. They worry that their parent can die of 'getting stressed' and so they will restrict their behaviour so that the parent will remain calm, which the child believes will control their parent's illness. Some children may also engage in a series of social experiments to see if they notice a connection between the way they act and their parent's condition.

These children often learn at an early age how to express 'love' as 'care' and to put it into practice. Many of them are also forced into the role of caring for their parent, and they may begin to believe that if they do a good job then the parent will no longer need to worry about their condition. The danger of this is that they may go on to develop a sense that they can do anything. A lot of this understanding also depends on the age of the child. Some parents may feel a lot of guilt about not being able to fulfil their daily responsibilities, and during times when they are more in control of their illness or drug-taking they may try to overcompensate or to make it up to the child by over-indulging them. This can be quite damaging psychologically, as the child sees this 'feast or famine' type of approach to parent–child relationships and may use it when he or she becomes a parent.

Parents who are infirm may also feel guilty when they are not able to go outdoors to buy treats for their child, believing that they are not making them 'happy'. If the child has a successful period of foster care and is returned to the parents, some parents may express jealousy that they can't compete with a foster carer because they cannot buy their children the things that foster carers can, when what children actually want from their parents are things that money cannot buy, like safety, security, a sense of belonging, a hug, a kiss, or for the parent to stroke or brush their hair. Many of these children will be bottling up their feelings about their situation and begin to become so afraid of how they may erupt as it builds up inside. When they reach a safe and secure place like school or a foster placement, they may show intense feelings of rage and non-compliance, or cry easily to let the bottled-up feelings out.

Mental health issues for abused children

Some of the effects of abuse will be short-term, and some will be long-term. Table 6.1 shows the most common signs and effects of child abuse. However, every child is an individual because each birth is unique physically and psychologically. This fact, among others, will mean that even individual siblings who have experienced an abusive upbringing may process their experiences in different ways. It is important, therefore, to look at what is distinctive about child (a) compared to child (b), rather than expect identical reactions. Some children will try to bottle their distress up inside and become withdrawn and anxious, while others will draw attention to their pain through violent behaviour. You are also likely to see other problems associated with PTSD, which is described in greater detail below.

Table 6.1: Common implications of child abuse

'Soft' signs of child abuse	'Hard' signs of child abuse	Physical effects of child abuse and neglect	Short-term psychological effects of child abuse and neglect	Long-term psychological effects of child abuse and neglect
Fear of adults	Bleeding and bruising	Scarring	Low self-esteem	Delinquency
Excessive crying	Sudden violent behaviour towards self and others	Disfigurement	Low self-efficacy	Aggression
Low motivation		Neurological damage	Poor linguistic and cognitive competence	Domestic violence
Poor peer group relationships	Sexualised behaviour and language inappropriate to their age	Sensory impairments	Hard to regulate their emotions	Child abuse
Anxiety		Failure to thrive		Substance misuse
Depression	Recurrent hospitalisation or admissions to 'Accident and Emergency'		Excesses of internalising and externalising behavioural problems	Self-injury
Absconding				Anxiety
			Relationship difficulties	Depression
				Somatisation
				Difficulty making and maintaining intimate relationships
				Suicide

What is trauma?

Witnessing an event that is extremely terrifying and/or dangerous, such as a vicious rape or other serious assault, relentless cruelty, or a tragic accidental death, murder or disaster, is something that can happen to any of us. Such experiences can cause *trauma*, which is the body's way of processing severe stresses on its physical and emotional systems. Trauma (also referred to as 'traumatic stress') affects the way we may then go on to adjust and return to a more satisfying way of living. Many foster children have experienced trauma. A child who enters foster care may have endured a range of physical and psychological assaults. Some may be torn from their families, showing great resistance and witnessing violence and high levels of emotional distress. This may be the case particularly for children who are removed with a police escort. Chapter 4, you will remember, highlights the trauma of being removed into care. After all this, it may be that you do not have a smooth introduction to your new foster child. However, for many children, being in a foster home may be a wholly positive experience as the child may see it as an 'escape' from a life of enduring and **significant harm** (see Chapter 3).

How does trauma affect children?

We all react in different ways to traumatic events. Children may have disturbed sleep with bad dreams and nightmares, or return ('regress') to earlier ways of behaving, such as being clingy, or wetting and soiling themselves, or have intense feelings of worry and restlessness; there may be a deterioration in their interpersonal skills with adults and children; or they may say that they feel like vomiting, or complain of physical pain or discomfort; or their eating patterns may change drastically. These reactions may be seen immediately, or sometimes the child may not show the impact for days or weeks. When they do start to show the effects it may go on for months and be very disruptive to their life – and yours.

For children who are refugees or from families who are seeking asylum in the UK, there is the high probability that they have witnessed, or have been attacked in, a violent episode, or perhaps have seen their parents and relatives abused, tortured, and sometimes murdered. Many refugee children suffer from post-traumatic stress disorder (PTSD) as a result, and require treatment and special support. It is important to point out here that some of these children travel to the UK alone, with little or no information on their destination, or indeed without even being able to speak English. If the traumatic experience threatened the child's life or physical well-being, he or she may feel particularly stunned or powerless. The intensity of trauma and confusion is particularly high for this group of foster children.

Traumatised children who are in a settled environment will usually make an initial recovery from the intense feelings of shock after a few weeks with the help and support of people whom they know and love. For foster children there may be longer-lasting effects, because of the unstable relationships and the additional complication of the lack of a secure future. If the uncomfortable feelings go on for a long period of time, it is likely that the child will go on to have feelings of depression and anxiety that worsen over time. For other children, their response to trauma may resemble attention deficit and hyperactivity disorder (ADHD).

Traumatised children can have 'flashbacks' that replay the traumatic event in their mind. What they are 'seeing' and feeling is invisible to us, but you may observe that they begin to show intense or extreme distress. Because of the way it happens, you may be thinking that the child will start to cry and scream 'for no reason'. Also, they may have a low threshold for being startled by sudden noises, particularly sounds that they have memorised as being associated with the traumatic event.

The mental health concerns of foster children
The Children Act 1989 promotes the idea that services should attempt to maintain children in their own homes. One could therefore speculate that many children enter the foster care system when other services have failed, and hence will come from very worrying circumstances and have more physical, developmental and psychological needs than their peers. Compared with children brought up by their parents, children in foster care appear to be at higher risk for psychological disorders. Regrettably, the actual foster care experiences may increase or complicate psychological problems, because multiple and erratic foster placements are common for children who have profound psychological damage.

Many children within the foster care system are at significant risk of mental health problems because of their history of harsh treatment and neglect. Exposure to drug and alcohol abuse, both before and after they were born, is also increasingly common in young children entering the foster care system. Many children in foster care are members of minority populations and share a background of persistent poverty with associated family disruption, chronic stress and social problems. Taken together, these facts may mean that these children are also vulnerable to emotional and learning problems (see Chapter 7). Specific problems identified for foster children range from relationship difficulties, aggressive behaviour and emotional and behavioural disturbances, to depression and hyperkinetic disorders, which may or may not be linked to a dip in school performance. Foster children with birth parents who have a mental illness are three times more likely to have issues of mental hygiene than others in the foster care system.

Being placed in the foster care system itself presents a significant psychological challenge, as has been described earlier in this book; children must adjust to the effects of the range of traumatic events that led to their entry into foster care, as well as the emotional upheaval of the range of losses, and adjust to new families and living situations. It is important that you recognise that severe experiences can leave a child with confused feelings about leaving their family. A fact that many of us ignore or avoid is that uncertainty is a natural part of life. We ignore this fact because we think that acceptance of it can be disruptive to our lives, or that we will be less inclined to plan our lives. This point is very relevant for looked after children, and consequently we sometimes witness a foster child attempting to take control (see Chapter 10).

Disclosure

A **disclosure** is when your foster child tells you about an event that was traumatic for him or her. A child may disclose quite soon after abuse has occurred. For others it may take many years – some people do not disclose abuse until they are adults with children, or even grandchildren, of their own. When a child makes a disclosure, it may be an indication that they are taking the first step on the road to recovery. In many instances, the child may have told another trusted adult, before coming to live with you, because they wanted the abuse to stop, and, following investigation, a decision was then made to remove the child into foster care for the first time. By contrast, many other foster children may show adults around them that they have experienced a trauma through their behaviour, but lack the courage to give details of what has happened to them. Being placed in emotionally secure foster care will often provide the encouragement that the child needs in order to say what has happened. When a foster child discloses to you, it is usually a good sign that they trust you. For some children the recovery process is smooth (see Figures 6.1 and 6.2), but others may need specialist help.

Case study: Sejal

Children's understanding of their feelings about their life can vary from day to day, hour to hour, minute to minute. Their emotions are strongly influenced by their beliefs and their understanding of their situation and whether they accept the realities of it. In turn, their beliefs are influenced by their ever-changing feelings. Foster children may begin to feel very confused.

Sejal was 14 years of age. She was the fourth child in a sibling group of ten children. One of her older brothers and an older sister were removed into care at the same time as Sejal, because they both refused to attend school. They had also started to become involved in crime, violence and drug misuse. Her parents pleaded inability to control their older children. An older and a younger sibling had died, and Sejal's social worker suspected that these tragedies had had a significantly disabling effect on her mother's ability to adequately parent her surviving children. Sejal came to therapy with powerful feelings of defiance and loyalty towards her family. She expressed a belief that the social service department (SSD) was overreacting to her parents' situation, and that she would return home when the courts agreed that her parents provided adequate care. When the court agreed with the SSD, she reluctantly went into a placement, with the full expectation that she would return to her parents at a time of her own choosing. She became riddled with guilt about not living at home, yet at other times she also felt guilty that she had begun to believe that she did not want to live the way her family did any more. When told of the real prospect of returning home some months later, however, Sejal began to feel less certain about going home. She began to 'act up' so that people once again became worried about her, and to obstruct her return home.

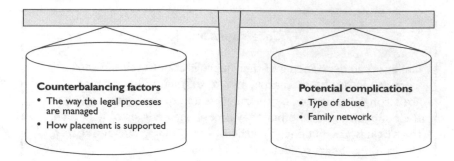

Figure 6.1: Adjustment to abuse or neglect

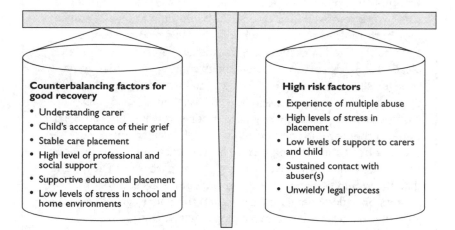

Figure 6.2: Risks to the process of recovery from abuse

What can you do to help?

Children can be as severely affected by traumatic events as adults. It is important that you accept that a child will be distressed and that this is normal. Foster carers can also help by letting their foster child talk about the event(s), or help them to relive it in games and drawings, if they want to. Actively preventing or discouraging a child from talking about the trauma in the hope that they will forget about it will not help. Although talking usually helps us all to adjust, it particularly allows a child to process and make their own sense of what has happened. Forcing them to talk about it when they don't want to is equally unhelpful.

Be aware that when you hear the child talking about the traumatic event (disclosure) you may also become quite uncomfortable, anxious, or distraught. It is usually better to state clearly that you are feeling their distress, as it shows empathy, but also to find a strategy for regaining control of your feelings – otherwise you may become distracted from the powerful declarations that the child has gathered the courage to make. It is important that, if you feel this way, you are able to access support for yourself. Discuss this with your supervising social worker.

As a foster carer you must be able to recognise trauma and to distinguish it from 'naughty behaviour', as then you will be better able to support the child's recovery, and also to know when you may need to seek professional advice to help the child.

Therapy or **counselling** may help the young person to feel better if they feel understood and emotionally secure with their therapist or counsellor. The focus of any help will be to support the child by building a trusting relationship again, and enabling them to gradually dilute their negative feelings about the abuse and increase their feelings of self-worth and hope. Foster carers will be able to see the improvements in the way that the young person communicates, or in a change in their attitude to socialising, or in their schoolwork, but this can sometimes take a great deal of time. Sometimes, the child may even become more unsettled before they are able to recover.

Other mental health concerns for looked after children

Depression

Anyone who has ever seen a movie or a soap opera will know that we can experience a whole range of emotions in very short periods of time. Positive and negative emotions are a natural part of being human. Depression is a mental health disorder which occurs when sad emotions become overwhelming. A person who is depressed may find it hard to feel motivated or excited about their life. Everything feels burdensome – even talking or moving their body. They may have strong feelings of inadequacy, be downhearted and easily stressed. They may battle with intense feelings of guilt or worry or loneliness. Depression can also show itself in other ways, for example self-harm, substance misuse, eating disorders, and even bullying.

Only in the last 20 years or so has childhood depression been taken seriously. This is because it is a problem that has been linked to a gradual rise in parasuicide (attempted suicide) and therefore has become of great interest from a psychological and mental health perspective. Depressed children may show a dull or gloomy look on their face. This is connected to a feeling deep down of helplessness, worthlessness and hopelessness. With mild depression the child may show a lack of energy, and this is often mistaken for idleness, especially in teenagers. There may be a significant change in their eating and/or sleep patterns, or in the quality or volume of schoolwork. They may ignore or withdraw from friends. They may become easily annoyed or over-sensitive, or there may be a sudden increase in dangerous behaviour, for example drug or alcohol misuse, jumping from buildings or railway lines, or delinquency. It is important to recognise that childhood depression may not present in the same way as depression in adults, and it is always best to seek further psychological assessment if there is concern.

Bereavement

One of the main causes of depression is the death of a loved one. For some looked after children it may be their primary caregiver, i.e. a parent or grand-parent, who has died. Studies on bereavement show that these powerful feelings of grief are similar to feelings of loss. However, the main distinction between bereavement and loss is that bereavement will nearly always involve a traumatic event. A bereaved child may show their grief in a range of ways. You may see a lower output at school, a higher level of irritability, and aggressive behaviour. If a child goes into care as a consequence of the death of their primary carer, it is a double loss for the child if they also lose the social support system known as 'the family'. You may also see substance misuse; that is, inappropriate or excessive consumption of prescribed and non-prescribed drugs, alcohol and/or smoking in an attempt to numb the pain of the bereavement.

Deliberate self-harm (DSH)

A young person can have intense thoughts of ending their life ('suicidal ideation') as a response to a bereavement of a dearly loved one, believing that they would feel a sense of comfort if they were re-united with the deceased. For this reason, a bereaved child being received into care is potentially at risk for deliberate self-harm. However, for non-bereaved children, DSH may be considered by a young person who has a chronic and/or painful illness (e.g. asthma or arthritis). Persistent arguments with friends, parents and/or carers, social workers or teachers, and having low self-worth, are also indica-tors of a likelihood to self-harm. The overall rate of successful suicide is low, but as a mental health concern parasuicide is relatively high in adolescence. It is more likely in girls than boys, but in adulthood this pattern reverses. It is extremely rare in young children. There is a relatively high incidence of a young person deliberately self-harming on many occasions before any suicide attempt is first made, for example cutting veins in their arms. There is a generally higher incidence of self-poisoning (overdoses) and then self-strangulation (hanging).

What can you do to help?

Every young person who attempts suicide should be referred for an immediate mental health assessment. Managing the mental health of looked after children should not be seen as the work of foster carers in isolation. Multi-agency support is even more essential for children expressing a desire to end their life or harm themselves. Make sure there is no easy access to medication or poisons in your home. Children need a close relationship in order to believe in themselves again. They need time to be with someone who is completely emotionally available (open and non-judgemental) to them. It is crucial that there is someone who can find time to be emotionally available to the young person, as it is vital that they do not think that this person wants something from them in return. Help them to find this person, who may be you, a family member, a teacher or therapist. Communicate to the child that they are valued and discuss an immediate referral with your social worker or the child's social worker if you feel out of your depth. Psychiatrists can prescribe medication such as anti-depressants in amounts that won't allow an overdose, and this should be coupled with talking therapy. Research shows that this can be successfully dealt with by **CAMHS** professional teams, but you can also provide direct help by getting the young person involved in other activities, such as shopping, sports and going to the gym.

Self-attitudes

It has been established for a long time that positive self-attitudes are the template for good mental health (Coopersmith 1967). For looked after children it is a crucial area, as movement of placement and recurrent family disruption, for example inconsistent contact and time spent in and out of care, may leave the child unable to develop a firm sense of self that is positive. The young person can experience rejection, lack of love and care, no friendships, no healthy relationships, neglect, and few physical possessions or lack of stimulation. Many have seen a lot of violence and become 'troublemakers', or may have experienced a failure to protect, as a result of which they desperately want to please others, and so become overly obliging. It is therefore unsurprising that children with such self-belief become the target of bullies.

Bullying

Bullying as a form of abuse is, sadly, now a fact of modern life. It affects both adults and children. The intention of a bully is to intimidate and humiliate a person who they believe is weaker or inferior to them. Bullying can include many different types of behaviour, from nonverbal behaviour, such as staring and laughing with the intent to ridicule, to violent assault. A victim of bullying can feel terrified, distressed, depressed and worthless. They may not want to tell anybody because they feel so bad about what is happening to them and their own inability to control it. Sometimes the victim becomes the bully as a defensive strategy, or because of their experience of their home life. It's important that the child is encouraged to work hard *not* to believe that they are inferior in any way. If the bullying is happening at school, teachers can and should stop the bullying. A child who is being bullied may not want to go to school or to leave the house.

School refusal

There are many emotional reasons why a child may begin to refuse school. Sometimes it is linked to a stressful or humiliating incident in school with a teacher or another child; or it may be due to bullying; or it may be due to a family problem such as domestic violence, or otherwise to wanting to care for or protect a parent or a sibling; or it may be due to the child's poor academic skills or lack of self-confidence. It is still not uncommon for school refusal to be linked to an undiagnosed, specific learning disability such as dyslexia. School refusal, and many other school-related issues, can become a big issue for a foster carer, particularly if they are employed outside of the home. There is more detailed information on school refusal and what you can do about school-related issues in Chapter 7.

Conduct disorder (severe behaviour problems)

Disobedience (non-compliant behaviour) is probably the most common childhood problem. All children will be disobedient at some time or another. Despite this fact, it is the main source of frustration amongst parents and carers. However, when this behaviour becomes the child's usual way of behaving it can become a serious problem, as the child is then 'out of control'. Some psychiatrists describe a condition where a child has a persistent pattern of uncooperative, antagonistic and outright rebellious behaviour toward authority figures that has a serious effect on the youngster's daily life. They refer to this condition as oppositional defiant disorder (ODD), which may include regular and excessive tantrums, open defiance and constant refusals to comply with adult instructions, and wilful, provocative misbehaviour. Younger children use such behaviour with the intention of manipulating people to get what they want, and they will often use 'pester-power', loud, enduring screaming, crying and breath-holding, throwing themselves on the floor or crashing and banging into furniture or walls. As they get older they may begin to behave in a way that is even more psychologically demanding on the carer, for example persistent lying, stealing small or personal objects, and damaging their own or other people's property.

What can you do to help?

The carer as the main 'therapist' is the best person to tackle non-compliant behaviour, since they are the one who is able to give direct support to reduce the non-compliant behaviour. The aim is to reduce the undesired behaviour and increase the desired behaviour by using a combination of positive (e.g. rewards) and negative (e.g. time-out) reinforcers. This is broadly known as the 'ABC' approach to behaviour management. This area is usually covered in your initial training, with additional follow-up sessions. If, however, the behaviour is severe or seriously destabilising to your family life, you may wish to ask for advice from a health visitor or psychologist. It is also vital to carefully consider the 'negative' reinforcers in relation to the child. For example, while 'time out' is quite appropriate for some children, for more distressed/vulnerable children, especially those with attachment disorders, 'time in' is more appropriate. 'Time in' involves setting a time (up to an hour) when the carer will focus their energy on a solution-focused discussion with the child. It is important that any other children that reside in the house have adult supervision during the period of 'time in'.

When a child is more often than not directly resistant to adult control, he or she is described as having a conduct disorder. Such a child will show a range of uncooperative and sometimes antisocial behaviours – maybe even criminal acts.

Delinquency (illegal and antisocial behaviour)
Young people who commit offences and are in contact with the youth justice system are more likely to have experienced some kind of mental health difficulty. Their offending behaviour is often as damaging to themselves as it is to others around them. Their offending behaviour is also often a way of dealing with their feelings of abandonment, resentment and rejection. Many

of these young people may lack empathy for the victims of their crimes because they are mirroring their own personal experiences of neglect and abuse. By this we mean that, in the young offender's mind, their victims are given a sample of the dreadful things that were perhaps done to them. Evidence of this can be seen in re-offending behaviour: they do not believe that there is anything 'wrong' with what they are doing, for example drug use and joy-riding, if it means having fun to them, while burglary or street robbery may mean to them that they have extra cash to spend. It is also important for carers to be familiar with the local youth culture, so as to be able to understand the looked after child's attraction to criminal behaviour.

Case study: Jamie

'I have to be a winner'...

The above comment, made by Jamie, a 13-year-old lad, transformed the therapeutic relationship he had been developing with his therapist. Jamie was in care owing to a nearly year-long period of harsh physical abuse. He had been to six care placements in two years, leaving exasperated carers in his wake. This diminutive, smiling, amiable child did not just want to be a winner – he *had* to be a winner. Jamie was ultimately saying that he had lost faith and confidence in adults' ability to position him as a 'winner' by advancing and supporting his interests. Issues related to trust (or lack of it) featured high on the list of themes that threaded through his therapy. The second dominant theme was the imbalance of his friendship skills, in that attracting and making friends was of greater importance to him than maintaining friendships. This young person could always be a 'winner' if he set himself such superficial goals: anyone who has been in a long-term relationship will know that it is far easier to attract and develop an intimate relationship than to sustain one. This is the simple reason why most adults are more likely to have a higher number of short-term relationships than committed long-term ones – that is, more boyfriends/girlfriends than cohabiting partners or spouses. The lad was also communicating that he saw his relationships as battles, competitions with power dynamics that he must control at all costs – and blow the consequences. This teenager's simple comment was a bit of a Pandora's box, because it was intended to make adults aware that this need to be in control, to be number one, to be 'top dog' was one that he was prepared to pursue with all his energy; and consequently it led him into numerous fights at school and in his community. Jamie was communicating to adults that he did not want and would not accept being dominated and controlled. This lad had all of the worrying behaviour that concerns responsible adults:

- acts of bravado, risk-taking behaviour
- threatening and actual violent behaviour
- staying out late
- being relaxed about or unmotivated towards schoolwork
- stealing
- lying
- sexualised behaviour
- criminal behaviour.

He spared his carers the headache of having to deal with his reluctance to clean up his mess, and also the irritation of receiving and overhearing constant, indiscriminate profanities. However, all the carers had high levels of anxiety about different combinations of Jamie's behaviours. This highlights the reality that it is not merely the behaviour of the adolescent itself that can be problematic, but also how the carer responds to it. Their reaction to the adolescent's behaviour is part of the equation. The main task of the carer is to make the child a 'winner'. By this I mean not letting them have their own way, or become unruly, but finding a way to operate on principles that preserve the agenda of enhancing the young person's self-esteem. In short, treat the child with respect and patience, and use as many supports as you need – whether literature or human resources – to understand what the young person is communicating with their behaviour.

Obsessive compulsive disorder (OCD)

The clinical definition of OCD is that it is the development of irrational thoughts and behaviours and relates to recurrent obsessions (i.e. persistent thoughts) that are acted on (compulsions). Phobias can be a feature of OCD. They can cause great distress to children and their carers because, if they are severe, they can become very time-consuming and interfere with normal

Case study: Cassius

Cassius's dad had been diagnosed as psychotic. Before Cassius was born, his dad had spent periods of time hospitalised as an inpatient. Mum reluctantly went to work against her family tradition to enable the family to survive financially. Cassius was referred to the child and adolescent mental health clinic at the age of 11 years, as he had developed compulsive handwashing. He was able to describe in detail which settings were less threatening, for example at school he did not behave this way but would in public or at home. Cassius would constantly remind himself to wash his hands at bedtime, and if he forgot whether he had done so he would do it again. If the thought entered his head that perhaps the towel that he had used to dry his hands was not clean enough, he would wash his hands again. Cassius spent very short periods of time in foster care for **respite** when his father was ill and his mother was exhausted. His compulsive behaviour was reported by his foster carer. Cassius was able to tell the therapist that when his father was in the worst state of his illness he would urinate in the kitchen sink, whether or not there were dishes in it. For Cassius school was safer because he did not associate the behaviour of psychotic adults with the school setting, whereas from accompanying his father he was aware that the latter would also urinate in public places. This was why Cassius's behaviour was confined to home and public settings. Cassius's handwashing was at its worst when his father was deteriorating to a state where he required re-admission, which would then psychologically affect his mother. The brief intervention was, first, for the mother and son to identify the pattern, and then to allow mother the space and opportunity to forgive herself for her hostile feelings and her guilt about wanting her husband to remain an inpatient. The family went on to accept that their style of living was fraught with expected anxiety whenever Dad was having a breakdown; the boy's thoughts about handwashing were replaced with realistic thoughts and practices concerning infection control. Cassius's OCD had an original 'trigger' that made sense. However, it spread as a technique for coping with all the anxieties he was facing about uncertainty. When Cassius was helped to understand how his actions made some sense (as a hygiene issue, because of his father urinating), and his mother was enabled to regain control in managing her feelings and his, then Cassius no longer needed the compulsive behaviour the way he previously had.

routines and social relationships. OCD can be very difficult to treat because the compulsive activities are often so integral to daily life, for example constant handwashing. People diagnosed with OCD can become agoraphobic and/or have panic attacks (see the next section on anxiety).

Anxiety

Anxiety can be described as a physical response to an emotional crisis. A person usually knows they are overanxious or having a panic attack when they begin to experience changes in their body, such as headaches, nausea, actual vomiting, fainting, breathlessness, tightness in chest or abdomen, or excessive sweating. These physical symptoms usually begin when the individual feels unrealistic worry or emotional strain when faced with a specific situation. They will need reassurance in order to overcome these intense feelings of panic. Nocturnal anxiety attacks, or 'night terrors' in younger children, usually occur when the child is worried in 'real life'. You will usually know that they are having a night terror because you will hear them suddenly shrieking, and you are likely to find them crouching or cowering in the corner of their bed, or rushing around shouting, screaming and/or crying, although they are not really awake. You will find more detailed information on sleep difficulties in Chapter 7.

References

Coopersmith, S. (1967) *The Antecedents of Self-esteem*. San Francisco: W. H. Freeman.

Hadfield, J.A. (1987) *Childhood and Adolescence*. London: Penguin.

Herbert, M. (1987) *Clinical Child Psychology*. Chichester: Wiley.

NHS Health Advisory Service (1995) *Together We Stand: A thematic review of child and adolescent mental health services*. London: The Stationery Office.

Useful websites

Royal College of Psychiatrists: www.rcpsych.ac.uk/info/mhgu

Young Minds (a charity for promoting children's mental health): www.youngminds.org.uk/publications/leaflets

CHAPTER 7

Psychological Issues for Looked After Children

Special Needs

Over the years, society's view of disability has gradually transformed from being exclusive to being inclusive. 'Inclusive' means that people with disabilities should be fully integrated into society alongside those who do not have a disability, and should not need to have completely separate facilities, or be denied opportunities to enjoy the same independence as people who do not have disabilities. There are various reasons for this: social policy, new laws from the government or challenges through the civil courts system (case law), and successful campaigns by various pressure groups to highlight bigotry and prejudice amongst the able-bodied members of our society.

It is now considered more appropriate to care for children with special needs in the community where their family live. This social policy has contributed to foster care being used as an alternative to residential care. Most looked after children with learning disabilities are in 'shared care' provision. This means that they have occasional foster care in order to provide **respite** (a break) to the biological family from the demanding task of caring for a child with significant special needs. However, some of these children will have been taken into local authority care due to **neglect** or a concern about the parents' capacity to meet the considerable emotional and physical demands of caring for a child with disabilities. Many of them have complex needs, owing to both physical and learning disabilities. It has been essential, therefore, to carefully consider the quality of care for these children because of the limitations to their physical and psychological development.

Because of their multiple needs, there are legal requirements of the statutory agencies to provide resources to address the needs of these children.

These are mainly covered in the Children Act 1989. The local health authority and social services department ensure that there are regular health checks (including sight and dental check-ups), that specialised equipment is made available, and that the child's medication is administered and reviewed (for those who are on medication). The local education authority has to ensure that diverse learning needs are met through the provision of appropriate human resources and curricula.

This chapter introduces you to the psychological issues for children who have challenges to their learning or their physical development, the potential impact on their schooling, and the various professionals who may be involved to support you and the child. There is also a description of some of the issues for children in the care system who have been living with parents who themselves had learning difficulties.

Learning disability and learning difficulties
Learning disability

A child who is described as having a learning disability usually has significant limits to the rate of development of their physical (as in movement and coordination), psychological, social and communication skills. Many such children are born with these difficulties or develop them in infancy (e.g. Down's syndrome, autistic spectrum disorder). Some of the conditions are degenerative (they get worse and more disabling as the child gets older), for example muscular dystrophy and cystic fibrosis. Some children are born with a combination of sensory and physical disabilities (in addition to learning disabilities) such as the conditions caused by the mother contracting rubella during her pregnancy. However, this is now very rare. Other learning disabilities may be a result of an injury or illness in early infancy, for example meningitis and encephalitis, or other infection or accident causing brain injury that may then lead to restrictions in the development of muscles and movement, for example cerebral palsy, or other effects on the brain, for example epilepsy.

Learning difficulties

Children are described as having a learning difficulty if their developmental delay is mainly related to a slower rate of development of intellectual skills and academic achievements. Some of these children may come into the care system because their learning difficulties were caused by some form of neglect by their parent(s). Examples of this would be children whose parents did not provide them with the appropriate level of physical care or stimulation for them to develop and grow, or whose mothers abused drugs or alcohol during the pregnancy, so that the baby was deprived of nutrients or oxygen while they were in the womb, for example children with foetal alcohol syndrome. Some children may have been malnourished after birth, with consequent failure to **thrive** that does not have a medical explanation. Other children may have special needs where there is a medical condition that does not usually lead to a learning disability or learning difficulty, for example HIV. Children who have a difficulty with just one type of learning, for example learning to read or spell well, or to compute numbers, are described as having a *specific* learning difficulty. These are sometimes identified as *dyslexia* (reading and spelling), *dysgraphia* (handwriting) and *dyscalculia* (maths). Other children may have difficulty in learning how to refine their body movements, so that they appear clumsy, or have difficulty in eating with a knife and fork, or writing. This condition is sometimes referred to as *dyspraxia*.

Some children have difficulties with concentration and self-control. In Britain this condition is broadly termed *hyperkinetic disorder*. In America it is called *attention deficit hyperactivity disorder (ADHD)* and this term is now being used more commonly in Britain. This condition has significant disruptive effects on family life as well as the child's schooling.

The psychological impact of a learning disability

The impact of the learning disability on a child really depends on how severe their disability is. Some children will have difficulties that will need up to 24-hour care for the rest of their lives, usually because they also have a physical disability where a surgical intervention will not help. However, those with mild disabilities may go on to achieve independent living, although some things will be harder for them to do than for people who do not have their learning disability.

Some children with a learning disability will have behaviour problems, and many of them may have low self-esteem because they are aware and frustrated that they cannot do as much for themselves as they would like to. Their frustration can be around how their disability limits their life, or it may be around the way they are treated by other people who do not understand them. Often children with a learning and a physical disability are treated as though they do not have their own set of fingerprints or personality – as though the label alone communicates all one would need to know about them. It is important that carers recognise the uniqueness of each child. Even though they may share the same diagnostic label, no two children are the same. Those two children will have different parents, and if they do not (i.e. if they are siblings), they were born at different times, and this will mean that their relationships to other family members, and to the world, will be different because they will be at different ages.

The emotional development of many children with a learning disability can be similar to that of a child who does not have a learning disability. This would mean that, although their understanding of some of the events that go on around them may be acquired at a different rate or in a different way, they will still experience acute feelings of loss, fear, anxiety, sorrow, love and delight. This fact is important because it encourages carers to see these children as complete human beings despite their limitations. With this knowledge, the carer can get to know a child's temperament and personality in the same way as with any other child.

Psychological issues for shared carers and their families

Some people choose to specialise in shared care. Some of these carers may have personal experience of caring for a disabled child in the past. Others may have a professional background working with people with disabilities. Being a shared carer has particular challenges, because shared carers have especially close relationships with the birth family. Some carers report that they often get more emotionally involved with the child because of their warmer relationship with the child's family. You may begin to feel like part of the child's extended family. This may also occur because there is a lot more physical contact and general handling of children with learning disabilities, and this increased intimate contact encourages another level of closeness that could not be developed in any other way. The relationship between the shared carer and the child can also be more intense because the child generally remains dependent for a much longer period of time than a foster child who does not have learning disabilities. If the child's condition is degenerative, you may have to struggle with powerful feelings of sympathy, fear and abject sorrow when you have to witness the child's pain and discomfort as they lose control over their minds and bodies. This process can be even harder when you have young children of your own who share the whole experience with you.

The social workers will probably have negotiated agreements about when you have the child for respite, and it is important that you stick to your side of the agreement. However, it is also essential that you do not position yourself as a martyr who has the child at times that are not convenient because you feel guilty about rejecting the child or the family. If you continually sacrifice your relaxation time, or your quality family time, you may end up resenting the foster child, and convince yourself that their family is taking advantage of you. Remember that there will usually be respite residential provision in your local area that can take the child in an emergency. If you have the child out of guilt rather than desire, it will change your future emotional relationship with the child. You and your family need to have your relationship needs met too, and if you begin to put more effort into caring for a foster child than you or your family originally agreed to, or more than you really want, the eventual emotional, physical and mental costs will be high, and everyone will end up a loser. It is more useful to keep in mind the hugely important role that you are playing in the child's life by genuinely welcoming them into your home and into your lives, while acknowledging and accepting the different feelings that you will have about caring for the child.

Children and young people with learning disabilities can be more likely to experience abuse, because of their vulnerabilities and inability to protect themselves. It is essential that carers are able to tune in to the child so that they are better able to detect any changes in behaviour and mood as one of the earliest warning signs of abuse.

Learning and development

As the child gets older, both parents and carers will continue to learn about the child and about the child's condition and its specific effects on the individual child. What is important to note is that there is a lot of help available for these children, which will help their carers to better understand and support them. The aim of such help is to maximise the child's opportunities to have a fulfilling life.

The type of help that the child gets is not only related to the specific needs of the child, but it is also related to the age of the child. Also due to the legal framework around children with special needs, there are some professionals who have by law to be involved with the child's care. What follows is a summary of the specialist support that parents and carers can expect.

From birth to five years of age

All pregnant women in the UK have access to a range of medical personnel in addition to their GP, such as *midwives, paediatricians* and *health visitors*. If the disability of the child is known before birth, there will be other services notified of the pregnancy. Similarly, if the disability is discovered shortly after the child's birth, a variety of services may be contacted, including *community paediatric nurses* and *occupational therapists*. There is also access to *physiotherapy* for children who need support with the strength, control and coordination of their body and their limbs, and *speech and language therapy* for children who need to extend their communication skills. If the child has a sensory disability, they will receive support from professionals who have specialised in working with children who are hearing- or visually impaired. Many of the children with sensory impairments will be supported by *audiologists* and *ophthalmologists* at the local hospital. There are also people who specialise in working with children who have been diagnosed as having an *autistic spectrum disorder*. Many of these professionals will work together in a service called the *child development team*, which is part of the health authority.

There are also groups within the community to support very young children with learning disabilities. There are specialist play groups called *opportunity groups* (sometimes referred to as *1 o'clock clubs*), which may be staffed by a *nursery nurse* and other assistants and are very much based on the 'mother-and-toddler' type of provision.

The local social services department will have its own team of social workers who specialise in working with children with learning disabilities. They will have been advised of the existence of the child by the health authority. A social worker will be attached to the child and therefore will be very familiar to foster carers, as he or she will be the person who coordinates the child's full package of support (which may include respite care).

The local education authority (LEA) will be another of the agencies informed about the existence of the child in the community. Most LEAs employ *early years specialists* – a small team of teachers and nursery nurses who are employed to visit the child at home, or in the nursery if they attend one. They provide *learning programmes* or *learning plans* which include specific advice and support on the teaching techniques and strategies that carers can use to extend the child's skills. The LEA also employs educational psychologists who monitor the child's progress, so that they can inform the education authority if the child will require special schooling, or special help in an ordinary school, when they reach statutory school age.

The LEA will have a multi-professional assessment of the child's skills and needs, and will decide what kind of support the child will need to continue to develop their abilities.

From five to eleven years

It is usual for children with learning disabilities who attend a mainstream school to have a special assistant to help them to make best use of the teaching, equipment and facilities in that school. If the child is placed in a special school, he or she will have a range of professionals attending the

---

Learning programmes

Research has found that children with special educational needs benefit from having a clear plan that lists what they need to learn and details the most effective ways of teaching them these skills. Many of these learning programmes are informed by **behavioural theory**, which gives clear and highly structured guidance on the *learning targets* and the corresponding materials, equipment and setting to support the teaching. Most structured learning programmes encourage accurate record-keeping so that the child's individual progress can be closely monitored.

There are many published learning programmes available through the early years specialists employed by LEAs, for example Portage, but many children will need to have an individualised programme tailored to their personal needs. Learning programmes can target any aspect of the child's developmental needs, whether it is intellectual, social, movement or self-help skills such as feeding, toileting or dressing.

---

school on a regular basis. For example, children with severe communication difficulties or sensory impairments may have visits from a creative therapist such as an *art therapist* or a *music therapist*. If the child attends a special school, it is unlikely to be in the child's neighbourhood, therefore the LEA will provide special transport to collect and drop off children to ensure that they are able to attend school.

Every school also has a school nurse and a school doctor (sometimes called the *senior clinical medical officer* – SCMO) who will coordinate the health needs of all the children on roll at each school, for example administering medication for epilepsy, monitoring oxygen use and cleaning the filters for suction tubes that one might use for a child who has had a **tracheostomy** (a surgical procedure that makes an opening in the child's throat to allow air into their windpipe). Sometimes school welfare assistants are specially trained to do these tasks. They will also be involved with feeding children and changing their pads during the school day.

Special equipment will have been provided by physiotherapists and occupational therapists where required. Occasionally children will have prosthetics (replacement body parts) which are monitored via the paediatric service based at the local hospital.

The educational psychologist will usually be involved with the review of the statement of special educational needs at the time when the child is due to transfer to secondary school. There are also specialist holiday playschemes for children with learning disabilities that provide a safe and stimulating play environment during the school holidays.

From eleven years to adulthood

The concerns for young people in secondary school will be around the continuing growth in their skills and their potential for independent living. If the child has a statement of special educational needs, there will be a multi-professional re-assessment of those needs, which will identify the precise steps that need to be taken to prepare him or her for adulthood. For some children, their special needs will mean that they require assistance for the rest of their life. Some young people will be able to negotiate a gradual transition to adult life with limited specialist support. Currently, there are specialist Connexions *personal advisers* who will be able to identify local employers who are suitable for work experience. They will also be able to advise on local educational provision or employment for young people with special needs when they reach the end of their school career. There are also supported employment schemes that are available for young adults with learning difficulties.

Special educational needs of the looked after child

Surveys over a number of years have shown that a looked after child is less likely to achieve well at school. There are several reasons why this occurs. First, if they are moved around from placement to placement, sometimes outside of their community and then back again, then, unsurprisingly, their education is disrupted. The child may become disaffected and lack motivation to attend school, preferring to avoid the recurrent struggle of making new friends, losing friends, and the effort of making themselves understood (both orally and through their behaviour) by an ever-changing group of teachers. There are also the severe mental health issues related to trauma (as described in Chapter 6) that can not only cause an emotional block to learning, but can also lead to multiple exclusions from school owing to extreme and dangerous behaviour. In such cases it is not uncommon for the agenda for learning to focus on adapting the child into one that is sociable and compliant before they can even begin to address academic learning. There will also be children in the care system who have developmental delays owing to neglect during early childhood. All in all, the foster carer will have a significant role in contributing to the child's learning, and will not only receive all the support that is available to parents, but also will have access to training from their agency.

Other special needs

Foster children are as diverse as children who are not fostered. However, there are some learning difficulties that put more strain on family life than others. Some of these are discussed below. The information on these areas is adapted from the Royal College of Psychiatrists 'Mental Health and Growing Up' series and Young Minds websites, and Herbert (1987). The website addresses are given at the end of the chapter.

Autistic spectrum disorder (ASD)

Autism used to be seen as a form of childhood schizophrenia (Herbert 1987). It is now seen as a *syndrome* (a specific cluster of symptoms). As the main difficulties are in the area of communication and social skills, ASD may be referred to as a 'social communication disorder'. It is probably simplest to think of autistic spectrum disorder as matched to highly unusual and concerning behaviour in the following three areas.

1. *Quality of social interactions.* An example here may be that the child has poor emotional literacy, so that he or she cannot 'read' people's feelings or notice or respond if someone wants, for example, to be left alone. They can also find it extremely difficult to use their own emotions and/or emotional responses appropriately – for example, they may laugh uncontrollably if hurt, or if they see someone else hurt. They tend to be solitary in their play because they have problems making friends and may not be motivated by social interactions with their peers.

2. *Severe weakness in verbal and nonverbal communication skills.* At one extreme, children with an ASD may have virtually no form of verbal communication. Deficiencies in *non*verbal communication may be lack of eye contact, lack of response to their name being called, and using an adult's hand to obtain things they want but cannot get for themselves (e.g. pushing the adult's elbow up towards a cupboard handle). Children with an ASD can be very difficult to understand and respond to appropriately. Children who are able to develop some functional language may still find it extremely difficult to initiate or maintain a conversation, and may instead repeat well-rehearsed but totally inappropriate phrases that they have heard on many occasions in a completely different setting.

3. *Very limited interests.* The child may show pockets of flair for an activity, and this may develop for a period into an intense obsession with the activity or object.

What can you do to help?

As a child matures, they usually begin to show some recognition of their social situation, and any window of opportunity to support the development of social skills should be grasped with both hands. The most successful methods are positive behaviour management, where the child is rewarded whenever they show any desire for social interactions, or any required social communication, for example gestures or language around greetings and partings. You may need ongoing advice from the Child and Adolescent Mental Health or the Community Paediatric Service, depending on how the support for children with ASD is delivered locally. For school-aged children any interventions will be done in collaboration with their school, under advice from an educational psychologist if one is allocated to the child.

School refusal (school phobia)

School phobia is an emotional reaction to fears about attending school. It is different from truancy, which is more about a deliberate avoidance of specific lessons in the school day or week. School refusal is less common in primary-school-aged children than in secondary-school-aged children. It is generally not as simple as a child not liking school, as many children do not like school, but still attend. In school phobia the reactions tend to be **psychosomatic** (there are accompanying physical symptoms and reactions). For example, the child may complain of headaches or stomach pain and appear genuinely unwell, or they may throw up at the breakfast table. School refusal will ultimately have an effect on the whole household. Adults may begin to have powerful feelings of anger or resignation, especially if they are working or if it becomes so chronic that the local authority begins to consider a residential school placement. The start of school refusal is often linked to emotionally charged experiences like bullying, ridicule, real or imagined harm, fear of academic failure, or an intense negative interaction or situation – such as feeling vulnerable, for example vomiting, soiling or wetting in school; feeling violated, for example being raped or having endured a sexual assault; or feeling ridiculed, for example being forced to read out loud although they were not a confident reader. Foster children may begin to refuse school if they have had multiple placements leading to many changes of school. They may be affected by their experiences of rejection, separation and loss, and lose self-confidence for making healthy, worthwhile relationships with both teachers and other pupils.

Case study: Daisy

Daisy, aged 13 years, was sexually assaulted at school by two boys. One of the boys left after the investigation, but the other was suspended and returned to school at the conclusion of his exclusion period. Feeling this was unjust, Daisy stopped attending school. She entertained ideas that everyone was looking at her, and eventually refused to leave the house alone. Her carer, who worked part-time, was required to accompany her on any shopping trips to buy clothes. After being allocated to a therapist in the child and adolescent mental health clinic, she attended her appointments only when her carer was able to bring her along. Therapy revealed that the powerful feelings of helplessness and injustice were compounded by Daisy's feelings about being emotionally abused, neglected and abandoned by her family. Her attendance at school gradually improved and returned to normal after the remaining male pupil left the school.

What can you do to help?

In the case of school refusal, there is a **systemic** need for full support from all agencies – education, health and social services. You may be introduced to an *education welfare officer* or *education social worker* for the first time, as they deal with children who are not attending school for long periods, for any reason. As this is a situation that involves all of the statutory agencies it can be very time-consuming, because you will usually have to attend meetings with various professionals from all of these agencies separately, as well as altogether. The process to support the child in getting back to school can take a very long time. Although there is a possibility of the child being medicated to reduce anxiety, this intervention on its own is rare. There are therapies that can be used that, can take several months of weekly sessions, and this level of time commitment can be frustrating for a foster carer who is working. School refusal can make a very secure placement quite unstable. It is therefore important that, if you begin to feel angry, you are honest about it with your social worker. It is only when you express your needs that support can be given. Your social worker may be able to arrange a day foster placement for the child, so that the placement is not put under too much strain. Everyone concerned will need to have a complete understanding of what is happening for the child. The adult to whom the child feels closest should take the lead role in supporting the child and taking them gently back in to full-time school.

Failure to thrive

A further consequence of physical neglect may manifest itself when an infant's rate of growth and development slows significantly with no genetic explanation; that is, no evidence of disease or organ failure. Such children are described as having a 'failure to thrive'. Often the child has been in and out of hospital for at least a year in its first two years of life, yet weight gain improvements made as an in-patient fail to be sustained once the child is back at home. Poor or no psychological contact or warmth will also be a feature of their abusive 'care'. Nor will they have had an opportunity for meaningful communication, verbal or nonverbal. There are several psychological implications for the child. They will tend to have an unhealthy look, which is the starting point of a cycle of poor social development. Their look, combined with an expressionless face that is hard to affect, plus a lack of motivation to get close to people, will make them uninteresting to other children. They will therefore tend to be solitary, and consequently have very little opportunity for conversation. Foster carers may find their emotional needs quite challenging, particularly because they are generally unresponsive to human contact and are very lacking in social skills. They may, for example, stare at people as if they are objects, and stiffen or flop when cuddled. They are also prone to depression and can burst into tears for apparently no reason. The medical evidence is that these children tend to respond well to psychological therapies, but may continue to have eating problems in both childhood and adulthood – these may become the child's familiar way of expressing uncomfortable emotions, so that they may refuse to eat when they are sad, angry, worried or frustrated. They will usually deny themselves food, but occasionally they may overeat.

Wetting (enuresis)

When we consider the usual path of child development we find that daytime (diurnal) urine control is gained before night-time (nocturnal) control. Some children have a learning disability that prevents them from ever gaining full bladder control. There are many medical reasons for wetting, most commonly renal or kidney disease, diabetes, seizures, infection or tumours. It is only considered to be a psychological problem if there is no physical reason for it and the child is still not dry after the age of four years, or if they go back to wetting after achieving control (secondary enuresis), and if it happens regularly. However, the muscles that hold back liquid waste products are among the last muscles to come under control in childhood. This is also one of the reasons why they are the first to go when a child experiences trauma, when they may wet themselves on the spot or even 'poo their pants'.

What can you do to help?

Enuresis is fairly common for children in the care system because, in addition to genetic reasons, they are more likely to have experienced a traumatic event and develop secondary enuresis. It is important to make a distinction between regular and intermittent or stress-related wetting. If you become worried about your foster child's wetting, you must go to see their GP. The GP can use medication if there is a physical reason. However, if there is not a medical reason, there are specialist clinics that teach carers how to retrain the child. Nocturnal enuresis can be the most difficult for carers to adjust to. Some people have found that restricting fluids, and then waking the child and walking them to the toilet before you go to bed, deals with the problem. For younger children, behaviour management techniques using stickers have also been helpful. Although it is burdensome, the most effective of all is the use of an alarmed pad, which wakes the child up if the pad gets wet. The alarm prompts them to wake up and go to the toilet. If you are given this device, you will be encouraged to give the child drinks in the evening, as a full bladder at night will replicate bladder control during the daytime, when they take themselves off to the toilet if they have a full bladder. Ultimately you will have to choose a method that works for you. Try all of them if necessary, as professionals have different opinions on what will help.

Soiling (encopresis)

Bowel control is the reverse of bladder control, in that a child usually learns night-time control first. As with bladder control, some medical conditions may lead to involuntary bowel evacuation and the child never learns full bowel control. If there is no physical cause, a child is usually taught to empty their bowels in a culturally appropriate place. There are two main types of encopresis. *Retentive* encopresis occurs when the child holds in the waste products, and eventually evacuates in their underwear when their muscles become very pressurised and they have an urge to push what feels like an obstruction out. This tends to happen just once a day. It is cyclical, in that the more they deliberately hold in their waste products, the more painful it becomes to evacuate the solid matter, leading to avoidance of emptying their bowel because it is so painful. There tends to be other undesirable behaviour associated with this, where the child will usually hide their dirty underwear, or smear the faeces on the wall or bedding, or they will smell of faeces and hotly deny that they have soiled. *Non-retentive* encopresis also tends to be involuntary, as the child will usually leak faeces onto their underwear and clothes, or their bedding. This may occur because the child is not paying attention to their body's signals, or they may be so engrossed in an activity that they ignore the signals. As with enuresis, a distinction needs to be made between *continuous* encopresis, where the child has never been trained to have bowel control, and *non-continuous* encopresis, where they lose the formerly developed ability to control their bowels. It is not always easy to distinguish between retentive and non-retentive encopresis, because sometimes when a child holds in their waste products and becomes constipated some of the fluids may seep out and give the impression that the child has diarrhoea. Encopresis is linked to trauma, but is also a common sign of **sexual abuse** (see Chapter 6).

What can you do to help?

Encopresis can be humiliating for both the child and the carer. It can be humiliating for the child because they are easily teased and avoided by other children, and it can be humiliating for the carer because you have to deal with clearing and cleaning faeces from unusual places. It can also become wearing for the carer when you continually stumble across soiled underwear in amongst clean clothes in drawers or hidden in the bottom of the wardrobe or under the bed, causing a very unpleasant aroma in your home. At times you may feel that the soiling is the child's personal communication to you about how they feel about you or your home. You may also begin to feel psychologically attacked by the child because, although you consider yourself to be reasonable and sympathetic, the child may continue to soil, and this may undermine your self-esteem because of the helplessness that you may begin to feel. It is, of course, useful to have a history of whether the encopresis is stress related and may have started following abuse or the move in to the care system. You must discuss it with your social worker if it begins to feel overwhelming. You should also go to the GP to get help as they will be able to refer the child to a paediatrician. The paediatrician can give straightforward medical support by assessing and monitoring the soiling. They may be able to intervene using enemas, laxatives and softeners, or give dietary advice. If neither of these approaches is successful, the **paediatrician** may advise on a behaviour management programme which, alongside the use of laxatives, may assist in re-establishing bowel control.

Hyperkinetic disorder (attention deficit hyperactivity disorder – ADHD)

These terms are applied to children who have pronounced difficulties in concentration, giving the general impression that they do not listen. They also show an unusually high level of activity. They therefore tend to be easily distracted and act without thinking. They also have huge difficulties with waiting for something that they want or taking turns in games. In Britain ADHD is diagnosed only when the child behaves in these ways all of the time, and not just when they are at home, or at school or out shopping, so that this behaviour is constant and does not seem linked to specific activities. (See also the discussion of trauma in Chapter 6.)

What can you do to help?

There is a lot of debate around this condition. This is because the number of children – mainly boys – who are diagnosed in this country has virtually doubled in the last ten years. Many experts are questioning why this huge rise should occur. Some experts argue that it is due to changes in society. We are generally more pressured and stressed by modern living, and do not have the flexibility in our lives to be patient with children, and we have essentially replaced high-quality interactions with our children with more and more attention to misbehaviour – a tactic that children commonly use to engage adults, so that a vicious circle is established. Others say that it is purely a biological condition that leads to deficits in the brain's ability to process information. Some will say that it is a combination of both. As there is considerable disagreement, the intervention is usually a combination of medication and psychological management using **behavioural** or **cognitive therapies**. The use of medication is also of great concern to some experts, who are concerned about the range of side effects on a child. Some are equally concerned about the temptation that it places on parents to find a 'cure' for their child's difficulties, with minimal effort to teach children alternative ways of behaving – indeed learning alternative ways of responding to the child. Some schools will run social skills groups to help children to learn, rehearse and practise the skills to engage with other children in a less oppressive and overbearing way. Experts are not certain whether a change of diet can affect hyperkinetic disorder, but some children may be more affected by certain foods and food substances than others. Many of the children diagnosed with hyperkinetic disorder will also need extra help and support with their learning. You may therefore be expected to contribute to a learning programme to accelerate the child's learning when they become better able to concentrate on class work. If they are given the type and level of support that makes a real difference to their concentration, they may be able to go on to lead a life that is free of the difficulties associated with this condition.

Sleep difficulties

Problems with sleep are one of the most common issues amongst children. For many children they manifest as a fear of being alone in the dark, or of wetting or soiling in their bed at night. Other children may have fear of a recurring nightmare, or 'replaying' of a traumatic event. Such children may become overactive at night to avoid getting sleepy. This burst of energy often produces what is called an *overtired* child, who can be quite miserable and exhausting for the adult to manage. Very young children can have *night terrors* that can resemble sleepwalking, or rushing around in their room, or otherwise the child may be found crouching in their bed, but they will also be screaming and genuinely petrified. However, they will usually settle to sleep again after a period of calm, close contact with an adult, and will usually have no memory of the event ever happening. With simple sleep-walking, the child will not usually be showing any signs of distress. For other children, their sleep problems may simply be due to the fact that they sleep for long periods in the day. Teenagers may have sleep problems because they are drinking a lot of caffeine or abusing illegal or legal drugs. There is also limited evidence that a child whose mother abused certain drugs throughout her pregnancy may also have difficulties with sleep. Some children have difficulty getting to sleep because they are worried or depressed. Alternatively, depressed children may sleep throughout the day as well as in the night. Not unexpectedly, a new foster child may need time to establish a peaceful sleep pattern, possibly owing to a history of abuse, or simply in terms of getting used to sleeping in a new environment. It is very important that good sleep patterns are established, because otherwise it can be very disruptive for the whole family.

What can you do to help?

The main solution to difficulties with sleep is to try to observe carefully what the source of the difficulty is and re-establish a routine that minimises or removes the issue and maximises tranquility. For example, if it is a young child that is sleeping in the day, then wake them rather than allow them to sleep until they arouse themselves. If it is a teenager, try to encourage them to find an activity to do in the day or in the evening like a youth club, or going swimming or to the gym. If the child is scared of the dark, try to use a soft night light and perhaps taped stories or a radio. These are also useful ways to teach children as well as help them to overcome their fear of being alone in the dark. Many younger children find the bath-before-bedtime routine sufficient to make them sleepy. Others may benefit from a warm, milky drink before bedtime. Whatever range of options you select, it is most important that they occur within a fixed bedtime routine. If you suspect that the child is depressed, you must discuss this with your social worker, who will be able to assist with a referral to the local child and adolescent mental health clinic.

Growing up with parents who have learning difficulties

Most children who are reared by parents with learning difficulties do not have any learning difficulties themselves. The capacity of the child to go on to grow academically and intellectually without the full support of their parents is usually linked to the adequacy of the support network surrounding the family. It is not uncommon for children whose parents are mentally or physically ill, are abusing drugs or have learning difficulties to contribute to the model of the general care practices of the family. However, the scope of their role can be determined by the level of social support that the family receives. Some foster children with a background of caring for adults may find it difficult to re-adjust to being a dependent child again, and this may cause some conflict or otherwise misunderstandings between them and their foster carer. It is important to acknowledge this and to focus on developing and maintaining a wide channel of communication between you and the child; both the child and your own experience as a carer must be acknowledged while you take on the challenge of negotiating new roles and responsibilities for the child in your home.

Reference

Herbert, M. (1987) *Clinical Child Psychology*. Chichester: Wiley.

Useful websites

Dyslexia Action: www.dyslexiaaction.org.uk

ADHD: www.addiss.co.uk

National Autistic Society: www.nas.org.uk

Royal College of Psychiatrists: www.rcpsych.ac.uk/info/mhgu

Young Minds (charity for promoting children's mental health): www.youngminds.org.uk/publications/leaflets

CHAPTER 8

A Protective Shield
The Multi-agency System of Care

Introduction

The tragic death of Victoria Climbié, and Lord Laming's subsequent inquiry into the failure of children's services to protect her, led to the development of *Every Child Matters* (DfES 2005). *Every Child Matters* connects to the premise of the National Service Framework (NSF) (Department of Health 2004), the Special Educational Needs Action Plan and the development of the Connexions (transition from child to adult) services to young people. The developments demand more cohesive partnerships in working practices with young people's services, including the health service, education, the criminal justice system, social services and allied support agencies including Connexions. When children and young people move from the care of their parents and enter local authority care, the system of people supporting them may increase in response to their needs. There is potential for the young person to experience a difficult mixture of feelings; provoked by stress and loss in the movement from birth family to local authority care. This transition in itself may burden young people with particular impairments and mental health needs, in addition to the very many reasons that may bring them into care. The 'state' may take sole responsibility for the young person, or will form a supportive partnership with the young person's birth family – parent(s), or kinship guardian. Responsibility for the young person is defined by law and stated in an *interim or full care order.*

The state assesses and attends to the needs of each looked after child through the collaboration of various children's services who work alongside parents or foster carers and/or the young person's social worker. This combination of professional systems is referred to in this chapter as the '**corporate parent**', and its collaborative work is likened here to what this book describes as a protective shield (see Chapter 2). Although the idea of **joined-up working** sounds rather dated and simplistic, in reality it is rarely achieved. In this chapter we argue strongly that enhanced outcomes for looked after children are achieved, as in any collaborative parenting partnership, through a strong commitment to the ideal of effective support of looked after children. This means that a culture and ethic has to be created where the various 'members' that constitute the corporate parent avoid working in isolation or otherwise alienating each other, as this ideal climate will better allow fractures in the system to heal.

The corporate parent – a professional protective shield

The collaboration of the corporate parent is rarely smooth or easy, but the importance of effective *joined-up* working is now recognised by all agencies (see Figure 8.1). Chapter 10, 'Moving On', gives an account of the continuing increase in research into the life chances of looked after children, and subsequent government responses through legislation that charges children's services with the duty to collaborate.

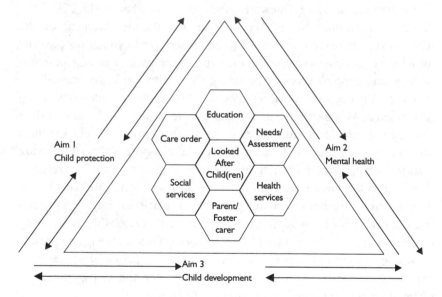

Figure 8.1: The corporate parent: professional subsystems as a protective shield

The corporate should act in a practical way to support the looked after child through everyday living, across childhood and adolescence, and more substantially to prevent or reduce impairment, poor development and mental ill health.

Child protection

The objective of the protective shield is for the relevant children's services to work together in an effective, corporate parent partnership to ensure the child's or young person's safety (child protection), and to promote their development and mental health. The overriding objective of the corporate parent, like that of birth parents, is to go beyond what is basic and enable the looked after child to **thrive**.

How the protective shield has helped

The case study that follows shows how the relevant services can work as a protective shield in response to the looked after child's circumstances, in such a way as to stimulate the child's healthy growth.

Case study: Tony

Tony was nine years old when he was taken from his mother and placed in voluntary local authority care, after a social services investigation found him to be severely **neglected** and emotionally abused. Tony's parents lived separately after a short but violent period living together as a family unit. Tony had a recurring problem with soiling and wetting at school and home as a response to stress. He was also quite difficult about bed times and his violent behaviour had become increasingly difficult to manage. Though academically able, he would procrastinate over the completion of his school work. This avoidance was subtly disruptive to other children, as he would regularly break their concentration with his meaningless monologues. As a result of this combination of behaviour, he was alienated in his class by the other children. The lack of regard by his peers spilled out to break times and Tony would wander around the area of the school playground watching yearningly as the other children played.

Tony had been living with his foster carers, Mr and Mrs Sharma, for two months when he told Mrs Sharma that his father had sexually abused him. This was Tony's first **disclosure** of abuse.

His incessant chatter in therapy revealed that Tony believed that everyone knew the details of his abuse. He was hoping that the strategy of incessant (one-way) chatter would leave no opportunity for children to engage him in conversation about the abuse. Avoidance was his way of trying to 'escape': from facing who he really is – a boy who has been sexually abused – and from hurtful and disappointing relationships. His soiling and wetting was also designed to keep people at a distance.

Tony wanted contact with his mother. His mother wanted unsupervised contact and overnight stays at home. Tony's social workers' role was to consider what protection needed to be put in place for him while he was in care, and what systems would foster Tony's best mental health and development for his future.

The first step toward doing is understanding.

Tony's social worker instigated a child protection investigation into the disclosure in order to assess the risk of **significant harm**. She contacted the local Family Protection Police Unit in order that they could investigate the allegation of the offence. The local paediatric unit and the Child and Adolescent Mental Health Service (**CAMHS**) were called on to make an assessment of Tony's medical and therapeutic needs. The school and foster carers were contacted to contribute to the investigations and assessments and to receive specialist advice.

The work of Tony's social worker, the police investigating officer, the CAMHS clinician, paediatrician, foster carer and school teacher designated with responsibilities for looked after children was devised as a direct response to the disclosure with the aims of protecting Tony from further harm, and minimizing the probability of secondary abuse as a consequence of their failure separately or together to maintain the stability of his mental health. Criminal justice for Tony was essential to the aims of each of the agencies individually, and the joint aim of the protective shield. This gave a clear directive for the agencies to carry out their duties collaboratively. The court appointed Tony a **guardian ad litem** who would be an advocate for him throughout the legal procedure.

Child development

What enables you to experience healthy personal development? Having goals, a role to play or job to do? Certainty in your future, or having your feet on solid ground, at least sometimes? Faith or religion? Reliable relationships – just a few good people you can trust, people who understand you because they are like you, in some way? What has made a difference for you?

Often it seems to us as adults that self-esteem or confidence is all that's needed for healthy personal development. For children and young people, who are growing and whose identity is changing and forming more rapidly, continuity, stability, certainty and familiarity with and within their peer and caring systems will more significantly contribute to their healthy develop-ment, their self-esteem and identity formation. This is even more relevant to children and adolescents who have grown up with trauma, deprivation or abuse. As significant numbers of looked after children move through multiple foster placements during their time in care, and also live with uncer-tainty regarding contact with their birth family, the school placement may function as the young person's single source of continuity: the familiar faces, friendship and the peer system. Perhaps this explains why for some children most effort is put into social and emotional activities of creating and main-taining of relationships in the school setting rather than a focus on the intel-lectual demands of academic achievement. For others the school curriculum is also part of what is stable in their lives.

In 2001 a school inspection team reported that, although looked after children accounted for 1 per cent of the school population, they accounted for 13 per cent of all exclusions. Learning mentors can be a way to provide a needed link and improved communication between the school systems that address the indicators of school achievement, such as those mentioned above.

Mental health

Consider how much who (and how) you think you are is referenced by the structure and relationships within your birth family network and your child-hood. It is so automatic for most of us that it is very difficult for us to imagine how a person forms a sense of who they are and how they are in the absence of such reference points. The Chapman family case study below develops the notion of a protective shield, and appreciates the significance of sibling group contact in safeguarding the looked after child's mental health and development.

Family trees, genograms and cultural genograms

Many of you will already be familiar with how to draw a family tree: that special diagram that shows your ancestry and your current family structure. A **genogram** is a visual tool used within a number of professions, including

Case study: Dawn

Dawn did not like school, although she loved physical education and excelled at football in particular. Dawn's mother, Carmen, had struggled to manage Dawn's behaviour since she was around five years of age. As Dawn turned 11, her struggles with her mother had escalated into frequent physical fighting. Their neighbours knew of them fighting and beating each other at home and out in public. A child protection investigation led to Dawn's registration under the category of **physical abuse**, and shortly after Dawn was placed in a children's home by social services. However, Dawn would frequently abscond from the children's home and from school, and would return to her mother. These visits would frequently end with Carmen calling the children's home to let them know of Dawn's whereabouts, and with Dawn arguing and beating her mother in protest. Dawn was eventually returned to her mother.

One day Dawn fractured her ankle as she was kicking her mother's door, and from then on she stopped playing football and refused to return to school.

Dawn could not recall a time when she had ever enjoyed school; she said she didn't like the teachers and the work was too hard. Dawn wanted to go back to school, but was really very sad that she would not be able to play football as she once had. Dawn showed her CAMHS therapist through role-play how a person can show their sadness through aggression, and so not risk losing face.

The school's special educational needs coordinator (SENCo) and education welfare officer (**EWO**), responsible for improving school attendance, joined social services and CAMHS to form a core group of professionals caring for Dawn and responsible for implementing the plan from the child protection conference.

The conference wondered whether there might be a hidden learning difficulty that would account for Dawn's longstanding disaffection with school. The school's SENCo requested the specialist advice and assessment of an educational psychologist.

The school provided a learning mentor who could be there for Dawn to turn to when she felt she wasn't able to cope. The mentor would be able to help Dawn settle back into school and to help her to find alternatives to hitting out in class when her anxiety rose.

> ### Using family therapy ideas in the protective shield – the Chapman family
>
> Ainsley and Eileen Chapman offered regular emergency and bridging placements to their local authority. They had three children of their own: Charlie, who was 11, Dillon, who was nine, and Kay, a little girl of five months. Kevin and Dorian Bailey are brother and sister, and were placed with the Chapmans after their previous foster placement had broken down due to Dorian's unmanageable behaviour.
>
> As Kevin and Dorian's stay with the Chapmans continued into a sixth month, the children's social worker grew increasingly aware of a number of dilemmas regarding their mental health and development.
>
> As time passed, with the children settled into the placement, moving them yet again to carers prepared to foster both of them on a permanent basis would have been even more traumatic for the children. The trauma could then have caused the children to avoid settling again and making new attachments. (Finding a single foster family who can care for a sibling group is a greater challenge than finding separate placements for each child. However, separating the children can profoundly exacerbate their experience of loss and adversely impact on their development/identity formation.)
>
> Perhaps supporting the Chapman family to keep Dorian and Kevin would be in the best interests of both children? Mr and Mrs Chapman began to envisage the impact of such a change on their family group and family life.

family therapy (Carter and McGoldrick 1980), to add more detail to a family tree, as it shows not only the bloodlines, but how traditions are repeated, or behaviour patterns are created and maintained for generation after generation. We can add further detail to a genogram, telling us about birthplaces, migrations, and the quality of the relationships between family members, and add information about a violent partner, or a history of childhood abuse, or mental health problems in a family. When a genogram is embellished with lots of information about the past and present behaviour of various family members, it can be referred to as the family's 'cultural genogram'.

The genograms that follow show the family systems for Dorian and Kevin (Figure 8.2) and the Chapman family (Figure 8.3). The *squares* represent males, and the *circles,* females. The line at the base of the genogram represents the generation of children. Above the children is the line of the

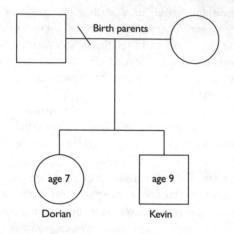

Figure 8.2: The genogram for Dorian and Kevin. The slash across the parents' connection indicates that they are separated. (A double slash would indicate that they are divorced.)

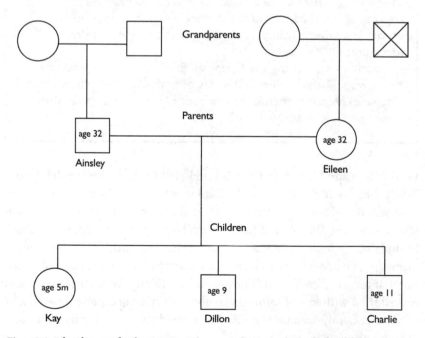

Figure 8.3: The Chapman family genogram. The cross indicates the death of Eileen's father.

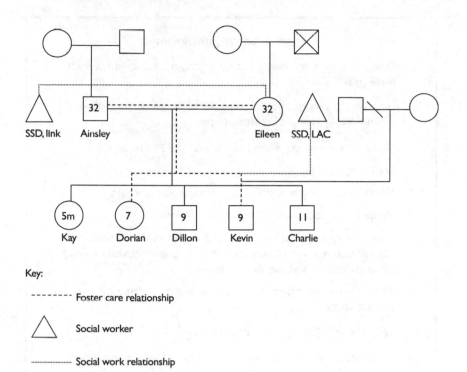

Key:

-------- Foster care relationship

△ Social worker

·············· Social work relationship

Figure 8.4: Dorian and Kevin's genogram merged with that of the Chapman family. The genogram of merged families includes the professional relationships with social services.

parent generation, and the line of the grandparent generation is at the top. And so it could go on, further and further back in time.

Figure 8.4 shows a merging of Dorian and Kevin's genogram with the genogram of the Chapman family. The result is a more complex picture, but also an opportunity to add descriptions and map out what are thought to be the differences and similarities between the two families.

With added notes, or even by sketching in a different colour, one could also show the special, exclusive relationship between Dillon and Kevin (a coalition) who share a bedroom and are in the same class at school. The 'special' connection between Dorian and Eileen's mother could be shown and highlighted. The genogram could show that Charlie has recently transferred from primary school – which he attended with Dorian, Dillon and Kevin – to secondary school. The genogram would help to show the Chapmans a picture of their household and family and indicate the impact of fostering on their family, and the impact of their family on the fostered children.

How to use a genogram

1. Take some time to draw your own genogram. Include at least three generations.

2. How would you go about adding detail to show the individuality of your family tree and relationships?

- Show where you are from and where you live now.

- Show any coalitions.

- Write in the religious affiliations of various members.

- Write in the locations of where people live.

- Show the type or quality of contact between individuals, e.g. regular phone contact, letters/e-mail or personal visits to and from various family members' homes.

- Show deaths, marriages and other events that changed relationships.

3. Talk yourself through your genogram:

- What words do you use to describe your feelings and your relationships?

- Which are the relationships that you remain confused about or cannot explain?

- Do you recall any family secrets? What are the family stories of pride and shame? What effect do these stories have on you personally or on your important relationships?

4. If you wish, write your thoughts on your genogram. Perhaps you can begin to notice patterns repeating themselves between generations? Perhaps you can notice attitudes or beliefs high up in your genogram that begin to make sense of the things people in your generation or the younger generations do, say or believe?

Fostering sibling groups

The importance of sibling placements is reflected in the Children Act (1989) that supports the desirability of placing siblings together, so long as such a placement is consistent with supporting the children's welfare. There is no guarantee that the placement of siblings will be free of difficulties – just as the new addition to a birth family can be challenging. If one of the siblings has special needs or disabilities, this can also be very difficult to manage well.

Whether or not it is problematic, fostering siblings can tap in to memories of successful or failed sibling relationships of our own. Although as a general principle it is encouraged to place siblings together, the prospect of success is influenced by a range of factors. Issues such as the roles that were ascribed to them when they lived with their parent(s) – for example, the man of the house; the helpful one; the caring/loving one; the nice-looking one; the difficult/troublesome one; the bright one; the dumb one – will continue to impact on their relationships in the foster family. These roles are equally likely to be familiar or alien to you. They may resonate for you in a powerful and unpredictable way and you may even find yourself feeling particularly drawn to the child who had the role that you were yourself given as a child; or you may find yourself repelled from a child in a sibling group that has the role of your most distant sibling. Even more likely is that you find it hard to make sense of their relationship(s) in any way at all. At times, this can be most pronounced for half-siblings, perhaps where one child is reared by a biological parent who was dismissive of the stepchild. This sibling, as a passive observer, may be viewed as the privileged or spoilt child by the (usually older) stepchild, and there are often strong feelings of jealousy that go with that. Or one half-sibling may have had a doting non-resident parent and/or their 'side' of the family accessible and available to them, while another child in the family had little or no contact with their non-resident parent and that side of their biological family. The children themselves may have strong views about being placed separately or together. If they have experienced specific neglect as a non-favoured child, they may yearn to be separate from their sibling, so that they will no longer have to share their carers with this sibling, who in their view has already been given so much more than them. If a child with such an experience is placed with a foster family that includes young children, they may begin to anticipate and look for examples of the biological child being given more favourable treatment than they are – whether it is actual or not. More commonly, however, an older child will have been allocated or self-appointed a role as carer of the younger siblings, and will find it hard to shake off this role in their new foster family if they are placed together. Often sibling groups are given the same social worker; however, the protective shield can be further complicated by the allocation of different social workers to each child, and the reality that the specific and individual needs of these siblings have to be taken into account comes into sharp focus.

Kevin and Dorian's genogram depicts a familiar western nuclear family structure. However, an increasingly significant minority of UK families share more complex structures with half- and step-siblings, and their consequent extended families and shared parenting. Like an elastic band, the notion of

The Chapman family (continued)

Dorian was struggling to make friends at school and often complained of being bullied. Kevin enjoyed school and made friends easily. Although he had admitted to stealing money from Dillon and Mr and Mrs Chapman, he expressed his wish to remain in their care.

Although the children and the Chapmans had adapted well to living together, the children's social worker felt it was important not to minimise concern for the children's mental health and developmental needs resultant from the events that had led to their placement in care. The protective shield, at this point, would attend to the impact on the children of uncertainty about their future in the placement.

The Chapmans wondered, given the different and changing needs of all of the children, how to split their time fairly among all of the children and still find time to nurture their own relationship. Mr and Mrs Chapman met with a family therapist who talked through their genogram with them alongside the life stories of Dorian and Kevin in particular.

Kevin was thought to have grown up in his birth family with responsibility for caring for Dorian. He effectively parented her and formed an identity as her guardian. The Chapmans and the family who had previously fostered the children believed it was their duty to act as guardians to both children and persuade Kevin to let go of responsibility for parenting his sister. This was scary for Kevin, who wanted to be good and accepted by his new family but didn't know who he could be, if not his sister's guardian. Perhaps Dillon had become a perfect model for him?

This change was also scary for Dorian, who learnt that breaking down the placement might also break down the relationship between her brother and the carers who would otherwise take him – in his 'protector' role – away from her. The protective shield incorporated the CAMHS therapist in order to support the foster family to work through their emerging needs.

'family' today expands and contracts between the traditions of different cultural groups. A professional adult system may make unhelpful assumptions about the importance of one looked after child for his or her sibling. It is important, then, to take into account each young person's wishes.

Young people should be offered support to untangle any rivalries and misplaced blame arising from complicated family histories that might unduly affect their sibling relationship. To this end, even hostile looked after sibling groups may find a personal sense of **validation** in the shared knowledge of their experience.

References

Carter, B. and McGoldrick, M. (1980) *The Family Life Cycle.* New York: Gardener Press.

Department for Education and Skills (DfES) (2005) *Every Child Matters: Change for Children.* London: DfES.

Department of Health (2004) *National Service Framework for Children, Young People and Maternity Services.* London: The Stationery Office.

CHAPTER 9

Assessment through Intervention

Many foster children are pleased and relieved for the authorities to find them a place of safety. In shared care, the provision of a foster placement is doubly supportive to the child and to the biological family; but some children may be torn kicking and screaming from their families. The level of the child's motivation for being away from their families may continually change throughout their whole time in public care, and most children in foster care show the signs of their significant needs, or their tragic backgrounds, in one way or another. Sometimes this is easy to read and to recognise. However, adults involved with children are often curious to know and to understand much about the cumulative impact of **neglect** and rejection on their foster children.

What is an assessment?

An assessment is a set of procedures that usually involve a variety of activities intended to gain reliable information that can be used in making recommendations on the best way to proceed or on the next step. Assessments are done across many aspects of our lives. A builder can assess the state of damage that may have been done to a property. A mechanic assesses what may be stopping a car from working properly. When we cook, we assess information that tells us whether the food is cooked thoroughly. An assessment of the human mind and body usually involves an extremely complex series of examinations, questions, tests and judgements. Our GPs will make an assessment of the seriousness of a medical complaint from the information that we give them in the brief interview at the surgery, and/or by observing and examining the wound or any other symptoms. However, you will know that there are many conditions that your GP cannot assess in this way, and these may require more in-depth exploration from a specialist.

What does assessment through intervention mean?

An assessment of someone's psychological and/or emotional status is in some ways more complex than the assessment of physical conditions, because it relies on the **perceptions** and comments of many people who will all have unique experiences of the person being assessed. Social psychologists have been studying the effect of factors such as the sex, age, **ethnicity**, appearance, accent or dialect of the assessor on the person being assessed (and vice versa) for many decades. The person being assessed may demonstrate external reactions to such characteristics of the assessor such as their age, ethnicity, gender, appearance, sexuality, accent...etc. Sometimes their reactions can be internal, and can become very distracting and disruptive to the assessment process. Researchers have also studied the extent to which individual perceptions on the part of the person being assessed influence their response to the assessor. If the person being assessed perceives the assessor as cold and distant, or warm and understanding, or judgemental or non-judgemental, for example, this potentially affects the way the person being assessed participates in the assessment. Similarly, their overall experience of the assessment will influence their level of confidence in the findings and conclusions of the assessment.

For this and many other reasons, practitioners now favour what is called 'assessment over time' or 'assessment through intervention'. An assessment that is conducted over time will usually involve the assessor setting different tasks throughout the assessment, and/or giving various tests during the assessment period, or may involve a series of observations or conversations. This model enables the relationships between the assessor and those who are being assessed to develop sufficiently well to increase the probability that they will understand one another better than could be expected if the assessment were done using a 'one-off' model. A one-off assessment occurs when a person or group of people is assessed and the findings, conclusions and recommendations are formulated after a single interaction. One-off assessments may also consist of a test or range of tests that are conducted during a single interview. This does not mean that one-off assessments are not useful, but that assessors are able to collect a much improved quality of information with an assessment through intervention. You should be careful, therefore, not to dismiss the findings of a one-off assessment out of hand. The fact that it does not tell you *everything* about a child or family does not mean that it cannot tell you *anything*.

Although the foster child's social worker or your supervising social worker will share some general information about the child that they intend to place with you, it is quite rare for a foster carer to have an opportunity to read an earlier, comprehensive assessment of a foster child. It is quite possible that the child will be having an assessment while they are still part of your household.

You may find that you are also assessing the foster child over time. Foster carers are a crucial source of feedback on the psychological progress of their foster child. You will notice when the child moves from an unsettled to settled state, and vice versa; you will notice when you have a 'honeymoon' period with the child, and when the child begins to be a bit more demanding. You will notice the child's mood when they return from contact with their biological family. You will also notice when your foster child has acquired a new skill or competence, or when they achieve a milestone in their physical development. You will notice when the child can read a book from cover to cover, when formerly they could not. The type of assessment that a foster carer makes is generally more informal, as the assessments over time that foster carers are more likely to do will involve a lot of observations and first-hand experience of the child.

Issues of objectivity and subjectivity

If you were to meet the authors of this book, to sit with them in a room and have a conversation for an hour, it is likely that you would be able to form an opinion of each of us that was based purely on what you believed (and remembered) that you heard and saw, on how the things that each of us said made you feel, and on your memory and beliefs about how we each responded to things that you said. If you were joined by one or more other foster carers for this hour, you would each have some shared views of each of us, but also many different, personal ones. The issue of *subjectivity* relates to one's individual and personal perception and viewpoint.

We are all expected to make judgements and decisions throughout our daily lives. These judgements are usually informed by a constellation of factors, such as our life experiences, 'facts' that we are aware of from books or other literature, our attitudes toward groups of people or situations, our beliefs about what is expected of us from various people, and our personal morality or integrity. Some of the judgements we make are based on our perceptions of the need to be accurate. In our daily lives we are routinely confronted with situations where we will make estimates or 'guesses' because there is no need to be absolutely right. All of these factors will assume different levels of importance, according to the anticipated impact that the judgement will have on yourself or others.

The prejudices and **stereotypes** that we hold influence not only the way that we perceive people's behaviour, but also the way we evaluate it. For example, if we were to ask 100 people to grade a picture of an angry facial expression, and we changed the skin colour of the face, more people would tend to give the 'black' face a higher 'angry' rating than the 'white' face. When we read about a mugging by a black person, we may respond to their colour as an indication of their criminality, whereas when we read about a white mugger we may respond to their 'thugness' as an indication of their criminality. Similarly, there are specific stereotypes of people of South Asian origin that represent the males as being domineering and the women as docile and homebound, and these may influence how we evaluate, for example, the family life of South Asian people. To give another example, people with 'posh' accents are assumed to be more intelligent than people with regional dialects or accents. Psychologists have for many decades been concerned about the influence of subjectivity on judgements made in the process of assessment. For this reason, **standardised tests** were designed to be a way of eliminating some of the effects of the assessors' **biases** on those they were assessing.

Standardised tests have been held to be a more *objective* way of assessing people's behaviour and skills – that is, they were originally presumed to sub-stantially reduce the relative influence of individual bias, prejudice and per-ceptions on the assessment process. This is an illusion in the sense that, when an assessor gives a rating, it is still based on their subjective judgement, unless the answer is based on a clear, correct/incorrect answer. Even then, some assessors may choose to give some people more leeway than others in arriving at a final answer (e.g. give nonverbal clues to indicate when a wrong answer is given, or allow them to change their answer). The decision to give nonverbal clues to one person and not another may be influenced by factors such as physical attractiveness and socio-economic status or class. There are also some standardised formats such as the 'strange situation' test (see Chapter 4) that are based on observations of raters. Again, this is ultimately a subjective process. Despite these drawbacks, standardised tests still have a limited usefulness in contributing to a *developing* picture of the person being assessed. Because we understand their limitations, in modern times tests tend to be only *part* of a comprehensive assessment.

Issues about testing

The use of tests is now a regular part of our lives. We have tests to show the condition of our minds and bodies, as well as for social and legal reasons such as the MOT (vehicle condition check), tests of driving proficiency, or swimming/lifesaving skills, and end-of-course exams. Tests that form a part of psychological assessments are usually standardised tests, which means that research has been done with a random group of people, and their scores on the tests have been subjected to a statistical procedure that organises the scores according to what the 'average' range would be expected to be, as well as the 'below-average' and 'above-average' range of scores. For some tests, obtaining a below-average score can be seen as a 'good' thing – for example, if it is a test of psychological disturbance. Conversely, obtaining a below-average score could be seen as a 'bad' thing – for example, if it is a test of intellectual skills. Some tests of psychological disturbance group the scores into categories of 'normal', 'borderline' and 'abnormal'. These groupings are aimed to indicate those people who have severe difficulties and those who do not. The people whose scores indicate an abnormal level of disturbance are usually the people who are offered the most direct help.

There are many issues about testing that mean that the results are not always trusted by the people who are assessed (or, in the case of children, by the people who know them very well). This is because ordinary people refute the assumption that a single test or a set of numbers can possibly describe a unique individual accurately.

Why are looked after children assessed?

Much has been written about potential adverse outcomes for foster children and their various needs. There are statutory obligations for agencies such as the NHS, the SSD and the LEA to provide assessments of these needs. What follows are descriptions of the breadth of assessments that a foster child may be subjected to in order to clarify, identify and recommend what best meets their needs.

The health services

There is a clear expectation that all foster children will have regular medical checks, including growth, dental and sight tests. This process does, however, rely on the cooperation of both the foster carer and the social worker in presenting the child for these various check-ups. The foster child must also be registered with a general practitioner to coordinate their medical needs.

The Child and Adolescent Mental Health Service (**CAMHS**) may also be asked to make an assessment for therapy. This means that a trained clinician, or teams of clinicians, with special skills in providing a psychological therapy, will coordinate and conduct a series of meetings to give them some insight into the internal world of the child. They rely on the child's expressed thoughts or behaviour, and examine these thoughts and behaviour, sometimes directly with the child, or using a more reflective process by discussing the child's words and actions with colleagues. An assessment for therapy is essentially about whether the child gives some useful indication that they would value the opportunity to spend some time with a clinician who will support them in processing some or all of their feelings about their past and present experiences. Some children may show that they would either prefer or benefit from a creative or play-based therapy, while others may prefer a talking therapy. All of the encounters with a CAMHS clinician will be shared with the organisation, but otherwise will be confidential to the participants within each session (unless agreement is sought from the legal guardian to share this information more widely).

Psychiatrists conduct specific assessments to diagnose a range of mental disorders (see Chapter 6). 'Mental state assessments' can vary in length, according to the severity of the presenting symptoms. This means that, if the child's behaviour is highly unusual and their thoughts quite disordered, the assessment may take longer than it would for a child who has a less severe level of mental health concern. However, there is no formula for how a psychiatrist will approach a mental state assessment and, as with all assessments, one child may be able to engage with the process (and with the psychiatrist) much better than another child.

There are a few children in our communities who try to kill themselves; most of these will not be looked after children. When this happens the child is required to have an assessment of their mental state by a psychiatrist or mental health professional. This assessment is usually done at the hospital before the child is discharged. This assessment is done to ensure as far as possible that the social and emotional conditions that may have led to the suicide attempt receive an appropriate level of attention, and triggers the provision of specialist support that the child will need to restore them to a more positive mental state.

THE POTENTIAL IMPACT OF NHS ASSESSMENTS ON THE FOSTER CARER AND THE CHILD

One of the main challenges of assessments for a foster carer is to have confidence in the methods and conclusions of assessments made by medical and mental health professionals. Many foster carers are in the position of knowing their child more intimately than any professional assessor within the child's protective shield. In groups that one of the authors [Jeune Guishard-Pine] runs for foster carers, they have expressed many times their cynicism that the relatively short period of time that an assessor spends with a child could possibly create an accurate psychological profile of the child. Even more foster carers express doubt about the fact that in their written reports many assessors base a significant amount of their assessment on the

What is therapy?

Therapy is an intervention that is used in order to address some illness, deficiency or imbalance that is present in the assessed person's mind or body. There is a wide range of *physical* therapies that you may already be aware of, such as physiotherapy, speech and language therapy, hydrotherapy and occupational therapy. There is also a wide range of *psychological* therapies that are available, such as **counselling**, **family therapy**, psychotherapy, cognitive-behavioural therapy and art and play therapy. There are also *complementary* therapies, such as acupuncture, homeopathy and aromatherapy. Some of these are easily available through the NHS, and others are not. In the CAMHS, the clinicians will carefully assess the child in order to determine which form of psychological therapy would best support the child's restoration to good mental health. The number of sessions can range from daily to two to three times every week, or maybe once per week. Towards the end of the process, the frequency of contact may reduce to once per month. Additional supportive sessions may be provided to the foster carer on a less frequent basis – typically, weekly, monthly or bi-monthly. As part of the therapy, the clinicians will conduct ongoing assessments of how the child is adapting to daily living, and will share their ideas in a process called a *review of therapy*. For younger children these reviews will usually involve the foster carer and the child's social worker, and sometimes their teachers. For older children there may be a different process of sharing. The therapeutic sessions may take place in the CAMHS clinic or in a local clinic, school, family centre or foster home.

'evidence' from written and oral reports received from other people, whereas they (the foster carers) have an expectation of some unique skill or technique that experts will use to form the bulk of the assessment. Of course, this view is only partly true. It would be inconceivable – and erroneous – for a skilled practitioner *not* to take account of oral reports from people who know the child well. This is why we talk about a 'comprehensive' assessment which combines oral reports as well as reports of first-hand observations and verbal material gained from a series of interviews and testing.

A comprehensive assessment, however, by its very nature, can be time-consuming and psychologically demanding on both the foster carer and the child. Foster carers are likely to feel anxious, just as any parent will feel about being judged by a stranger who is perceived as an expert. You may feel, when an expert gives you advice on a different way to deal with your foster child, that they are implying that you are not managing the child in the right way. This may or may not be an accurate perception on your part. In either case, advice is given to enhance the work you are doing with the child, or to widen your range of options for dealing with the child. Some foster carers have also remarked that they worry that they are being 'psychoanalysed' when they meet with a therapist. Others have commented that they feel a pressure to give the 'correct' answer. The reality is that clinicians highly value the contribution that foster carers make to assessments, because of their unique relationship with the child. However, this is not always enough to stop carers from worrying about the impression that they are making on clinicians. The purpose of this chapter is not to feed that worry, but to reassure you that it is quite usual for us all to have these fears about how we will be seen by others who do not know us very well. Some of us will worry about this more than others. These feelings are useful, as they enable you to empathise with your foster child, who is likely to have to undergo many assessments and meet many transitory people. If the child becomes non-communicative, and this is unusual, this may indicate to a skilled clinician that the child is feeling assessment fatigue from being 'over-assessed'.

If you notice this in your child a good approach is to ask directly, or suggest that they may be 'fed up' with meeting so many different people who may all be asking the same questions, or questions that sound the same to the child. From my experience, the child finds it liberating that an adult is able to empathise and notice how they feel about multiple assessments. This is a particularly refreshing approach, because when a child does not answer an adult's questions, or is blunt or is limiting their responses to 'yes', 'dunno', 'ummm', or simply shrugging their shoulders, they risk being perceived as rude, and there is a temptation for the foster carer to tell the child off, or otherwise become irritated with the child.

Although some foster carers may find it difficult to question clinicians, it is worthwhile trying to meet the assessor(s) with your supervising social worker and/or the child's social worker before the direct assessment of the child commences, to find out how the clinician will approach the assessment, and to discuss any issues or concerns that you may have about the child, which you think will be relevant to the assessment. Some clinicians may even show you the room that they plan to use for the assessment, if it is likely to be in a special room in a clinic, or if they will be using specific equipment. This prior information may be useful in allaying a foster child's fears about a clinic-based assessment.

The local education authority (LEA)

Since the Education Act 1944, there has been a statutory requirement that all children in the UK attend full-time school between the ages of 5 and 16 years. Until 1972, as part of the development of the school curriculum, children used to be tested in numeracy and literacy at the end of every school year, with a special test called the '11-plus' at the end of the primary school years. The Education Reform Act 1988 recommended that all children are formally tested using Standardised Assessment Tests (SATs) at the end of Year 2 (aged 7 years), Year 6 (aged 11 years), Year 9 (aged 14 years) and in Year 11 (aged 16 years). The tests at Years 2, 6 and 9 remain; and there have been additional developments such as *baseline assessments*, which are required to be conducted by the end of the child's first compulsory term in Year R (Reception year). For some children this will be the end of the Autumn term, and for others the end of the Spring term. Schools are also encouraged to give end-of-year tests to children throughout their school career. Some subjects also give tests at the end of specific topics.

The Year 2 child will be expected to obtain an average SAT score of Level 2. Less able children may obtain Level 1, and the more able may obtain Level 3 in some subjects. For the Year 6 child the average attainment is Level 4, with the more able children achieving Levels 5 or even 6. In Year 9 the average SAT score expected would be Level 5, with the more able obtaining Levels 6 or 7. Children who fail to make progress or who make very small steps in their development may require special assistance. This help is usually arranged through the school, but children with chronic difficulties may require the support of a Statement of Special Educational Needs (see Chapter 7). Some children with learning difficulties will have levels of attainment that are classed as 'W', which means that the child is *working towards* a Level 1 attainment. Children with severe or profound and multiple learning difficulties may be assessed using 'P' scales which are pre-Level 1 learning objectives.

Most LEAs have a group of specialist teachers who help schools to devise effective ways of accelerating children's learning, or to apply the brakes on poor behaviour. Many foster children will need the support of one of these teachers to make improvements to their learning experience. Others may need the support of the school psychologist. Educational psychologists have specialist skills in making a better match between the child's personality, learning style and academic skills, and the learning environment, including the curriculum that the child is expected to follow.

All looked after children have to have a *personal education plan*, which is a plan of action to support the child's full range of educational needs. It is a multi-professional plan that requires input from all of the professionals involved in supporting the child's overall *care plan*, which is the responsibility of the social services department.

There are literally hundreds of tests that are available to assess children's academic and intellectual skills. Although there are far too many to list, information is given, in the 'Useful Resources' section at the end of this book, on useful websites and organisations that foster carers can contact for up-to-date information. However, the best point for foster carers to access this information is their local school or education department.

THE POTENTIAL IMPACT OF EDUCATIONAL ASSESSMENTS ON THE FOSTER
CARER AND THE CHILD

School can be a very stressful place for a traumatised child. This is because there can be a clash between the school's expectations of the child's learning and behaviour, and the actual skills and reactions of the child. About two-thirds of looked after children in England have a recognised special educational need (SEN). Educational psychologists are able to assess a young person's SEN, and if appropriate produce a Statement of Special Educational Need to summarise the SEN and propose an education plan. Many foster children do not spend much of the time available for learning in the actual classroom, because their behaviour falls outside of the expected boundaries of acceptable classroom behaviour.

A useful way to explain this is by observing the hierarchy of needs developed by Maslow (1970), which was introduced in Chapter 3. Maslow maintained that it is unlikely for an individual to be interested in satisfying their need for intellectual stimulation if their more basic needs for physical well-being, emotional security and 'belongingness' are not met. Another reason used to explain why so many looked after children have difficulties with school is that the common features of trauma are not consistent with the skills required for focused academic learning (see Chapter 6). Stressed and distressed children are more vulnerable to the sanctions of the school's disciplinary system because their behaviour often presents as disruptive and aggressive. There can also be a clash because the business of schools is to teach diverse groups of children adequate academic skills for them to become independent learners and thinkers, and teachers may feel pressured to exclude a foster child from classrooms or from school, if they behave in a way that may be preventing their classmates from learning.

The school's aim to develop children's intellect and learning is nearly always achieved in collaboration with the child's parent or carer. The foster carer is therefore required to offer support for the child's learning and to be active in home-based learning programmes to extend the child's academic skills – especially if the child has learning difficulties. Not all foster carers feel comfortable with the level of homework that they are expected to supervise for foster children who may have learning difficulties. Nor do they necessarily have the patience. In very extreme cases, it may be possible to negotiate for a computer to assist with tutoring children. It is also very stressful if a foster child is excluded for a long time and no school is found. In such cases, the fostering agency may be able to find a 'day placement' with a registered foster carer who does not work outside of the home. Many foster carers become strong advocates for their foster child if they believe that the school system is not as supportive of the child's emotional needs as they would expect and as the child deserves.

For shared carers and for carers of children who attend special schools, there can be clashes between carers' expectations of particular forms of therapy or a programme of teaching or support, and the education department's will or ability to fund private or complementary therapies. This is an issue especially if the assessments that the LEA has done do not indicate a need for a specific type of therapy.

The social services department (SSD)

The assessments done by the SSD pivot around the exploration of whether the child is experiencing **significant harm** (see Chapter 3). The SSD will also convene regular reviews of whether the child's psychological development remains unhealthy or is restored to a healthier state. While a child is in care, the assessments that you are likely to become aware of are assessments for:

1. adoption

2. returning a child to their parents

3. determining the best interests of the child

4. a review of the child's overall needs (as part of a review that is sometimes called an 'LAC review').

These assessments may be carried out by a range of local professionals, or the SSD may commission an independent assessment from an expert.

Case study: Albie

At the age of 15 years, Albie was admitted to the children's ward of the local hospital after a suspected overdose at school. He was discharged from hospital after a mental state assessment by a clinician from the local Child and Adolescent Mental Health Service. He returned to his carer – a single male – and a follow-up assessment was offered from the CAMHS. A joint assessment was done by the school, CAMHS and the SSD, and the outcome was that two CAMHS clinicians were allocated to offer direct support to the school, the foster carer, and to Albie. Albie began to attend the clinic weekly for a talking therapy (psychotherapy). He was able to communicate his inner turmoil about the development of his multiple identities as a sibling, a son, a foster child, an individual, and his sexual identity – all of which were vulnerable and fragile. Many of these issues are a common source of anxiety amongst adolescents, but Albie's determination to communicate his individuality had made him a target for wretched school bullies. The unrelenting bullying was inhibiting his restoration to good mental health. He started to write strong messages of violence and self-hate on walls and furniture, at any opportunity, both at school and in the foster home. The foster carer used his sessions with the CAMHS clinician to process the impact that Albie's extreme moods was having on his own ability to communicate successfully with Albie, and to enjoy the experience of living with him. Albie worked hard in his individual therapy to recognise that he was able to be himself, and to be tolerated. The work with the foster carer became focused on joining with the school to eradicate the school bullying so that Albie felt safer, more confident and less fearful about the whirlpool of feelings that he was struggling to understand and accept. This approach resulted in the foster carer feeling more useful in supporting Albie's emotional needs, and consequently more emotionally available to cope with Albie's unpredictable behaviour, which he was better able to recognise as adolescent angst.

THE POTENTIAL IMPACT OF SSD ASSESSMENTS ON THE FOSTER CARER AND THE CHILD

Foster carers can find SSD assessments quite emotional. It is very difficult not to get emotionally involved with a child who has become a part of your family. Many foster carers find it both painful and stressful to witness the distress that the foster child may feel when they have contact with their biological family, or when the biological family disappoints the child by not maintaining contact. Many foster carers have expressed anger and rage about the biological family's inconsistent approach to the child, particularly as they have to face the aftermath when the child feels doubly abandoned. For this reason the foster carer can feel perturbed by assessments that conclude that a child should be returned to their biological family. It is essential that you are able to find and maintain the best way of supporting the child on a professional level, particularly if you are not in a position to offer a permanent or long-term placement. If you become aware that you have strong feelings for the child, it is important that you are totally honest with yourself and acknowledge these feelings. It can become extremely difficult and excruciatingly painful for you to admit that you have powerful feelings for a child, and that these feelings prevent you from focusing on what is best for the child – for example, to be with their biological family – rather than on what you would like for yourself, and what you would like for that child.

These feelings are essentially linked to very profound feelings of loss. Some foster carers may feel that a decision to assess the child and the biological family is an indication that the foster household is insufficient to meet the child's needs, and that any positive conclusion from the assessment regarding the biological family's readiness to support the child is suggestive that the foster placement is deficient in some way. This is absolutely not so. You will be subject to annual reviews of the placement that you are providing, and it is only in this context that the fostering agency will inform you of any concerns about the care you are providing. The assessments for adoption or for returning a child to their family of origin are entirely separate from any assessment of the placement.

It is important, if you begin to experience grief reactions to the potential or actual departure of your foster child, that you acknowledge this and share it with your supervising social worker. If the child has not yet left your home, your social worker can plan the child's transition in a way that is sensitive to your emotional needs, as these will nearly always be mirrored by the child. Handled sensitively, it could be important for the child to know that they mattered to you enough for you to hurt because they are going. However, this always needs to be matched by the joy that you share with them about returning to their biological family, or moving to their 'forever' (adoptive) family.

Reference

Maslow, A.H. (1970) *Motivation and Personality* (2nd edition). New York: Harper & Row.

CHAPTER 10

Moving On

Introduction

Children and young people in long-term care are likely to experience a number of placement moves throughout their time in care. Moving on can mark the most demanding periods in the care process. At this enormously influential event in the young person's personal development, strong emotions are provoked in both the foster carer and the young person, and high-quality skills are demanded from the protective shield (the professional system of care described in Chapter 8).

Looked after children represent a diverse group with diverse histories and ethnic backgrounds, and they may remain in local authority care for anything from a few days to many years. However, the themes relating to moving on, and the importance of creating with the young person the best and most empowering experience of moving on, is relevant to all children in transition. Their destinations are equally varied: because of their age, some may go on to live independently or in a hostel, or to live in supported lodgings or with relatives. Some may return to their parents because there have been improvements in the parents' health or in their parenting capabilities. Support from foster carers at this time is crucial.

Bridging beginnings and endings

The 'moving on' of the title is at this point usefully thought of as a bridge connecting saying 'goodbye' to saying 'hello' between one home and the next. The process of moving on bridges all of the fundamental differences between placements; there will be differences in expectations, routines, proximity to birth family and school, and perhaps an ethnic cultural change in foster carers and/or the local communities.

Crossing the bridge can represent the notion of 'doing' change. We all do change of this kind through the act of living, be it through such experiences as loss, or moving house, or a change in employment. The impact of changes that we have experienced in our past shapes how we think of change in the present, and how we go on to do change in the future. The same is of course true for looked after children, who will bring their own beliefs, what they have learnt from past moves, their hopes and fears and coping strategies to their experience of doing the change and moving on.

It is important to understand that each one of us will have beliefs about moving on and what change means to us. Our beliefs about change will be unique because we are each unique. Our unique set of beliefs will shape, in a specific or special way, what we do when faced with change. Foster children who are siblings, who are taken through a similar process of change, from birth family to a shared foster care placement, for example, may experience the change together but will do the change differently…uniquely.

Our ways of moving on and doing change are mostly instinctive in that we appear to just do what we do without an awareness of the beliefs that guide us – we don't generally pause to tell ourselves why we are going to do things this way or that way, before doing so. Mostly we will act into the flow of a situation in the moment-by-moment unfolding of living. But our beliefs shape that moment-by-moment flow of living; they are woven in like a cross-thread that holds the fabric together.

Bridging the difference

The challenge for foster carers is to keep in mind what they have learnt about how children and young people manage moving on. It is of equal importance that foster carers hold on to their own beliefs about what moving on means and feels like, but hold on to those thoughts *lightly* and listen out for the unique **perceptions** and needs of the young person.

Embarking on a conversation about the things that we mostly do intuitively may seem odd. It may also seem odd to be genuinely curious about the things that we assume to know. Most people – adults, young people and children – may have difficulty in finding the *words* to describe what moving on has become for them. It can take practice, too, for a looked after child to think through, and then talk through, how past experiences have come to shape the ideas they hold now, and how they view the future. Sharing experiences of moving on with a child in your care can help, but it is important to help the young person to find their own words that describe what moving on has come to mean for them. This kind of conversation helps to create a way in to talking about how the young person would wish to experience moving on, and how the foster carer can respond to those wishes.

Depending on the relationship between the foster carer and the young person, the task of having this discussion may seem either straightforward, or unlikely or delicate. Foster carers can be supported by their supervising social worker in developing the skills for this type of process. In complex situations support or one-to-one work can be gained through a Child and Adolescent Mental Health Service (**CAMHS**) therapeutic provision for the child moving on.

It may seem more appropriate for an adult who knows the young person more intimately and who will be consistently available through the process of moving on to have these conversations with the young person. A member of the young person's school staff, class teacher, learning mentor or designated teacher for looked after children could also talk over the subject with the young person. However, school staff may be limited by the school timetable, and by holidays. The young person's social worker could lead this discussion, if not debilitated by the quality of their relationship with the young person at the time and the young person's perception of the part their social worker has played in bringing about the move.

Helping looked after children to talk about moving on will help them, to some extent, to address their fears and hopes about it in a way that enables them to build productive strategies, and also build **resilience**. It also helps the foster carer to work out how to respond to the unique needs of the young person in their care (or those of the young person they are to receive into their care). Failure to hold such a discussion may have unwanted consequences for the way a young person's beliefs, hopes and fears shape the manner of their moving on.

Marking the ending of a placement with a letter like the one written to Joseph in the case study below creates a real point of reference that enables the young person to remember their achievements in moving on. Joseph moved on from expressing his fears **psychosomatically** through bedwetting and headaches to talking through his fears, changing his perception of moving on and ultimately affecting the moving-on plan. The letter can help Joseph to remember his achievements and the things he was able to change (as opposed to the bedwetting, for example, which would be embarrassing for most children, and unlikely to be remembered in its proper context as an expression of real fears). Moving on can be marked with a homemade certificate, a celebration or a special card.

Case study: Joseph

Joseph's parents had been abusing non-prescription drugs and were **neglecting** Joseph's needs and exposing him to risks within the family home. Joseph was 12 when he was placed temporarily with foster carers in Bath, having been removed from his parents who lived in Bristol. Joseph's placement in Bath was short-term – until his social worker could either match him with a suitable local placement, or, if his parents were able to make better use of the support, Joseph could return to them. Joseph remained in Bath but had twice-weekly supervised contact with his parents at their home. Joseph's parents wanted their son back home with them. Although Joseph had been let down and hurt by his parents many times before, he also wanted to return home.

Six months passed and the temporary placement had become a settled environment, despite having to enrol Joseph in a new school, so that he lost touch with his old friends. However, his parents had made great strides in remaining drug-free – contact had been unsupervised for the last four weeks and Joseph had slept over for the last three weekends. Joseph's social worker told him he would be going home very soon. Joseph had always said he wanted to be back with his parents, and so his social worker was not surprised to see that he was pleased to hear the news.

The next morning, Joseph's foster carer saw that Joseph had wet his bed. He hadn't done this since he first moved in. Later that morning, Joseph complained that he had a bad headache and didn't want to go to school. His foster carer let him stay home for the day and used the opportunity to talk about moving on.

In time, Joseph was able to tell his foster carer that he had a mixture of feelings: he was happy that everything was better, but he was also scared that moving back to his parents would be moving back to the way things were before. His parents would have no reason to stay off the drugs – they didn't when he lived with them before! Joseph decided, as he spoke, that what he had at that moment was a really nice balance: a kind foster carer who played with him, lots of contact with his parents, and new friends who didn't know his parents. It was the best! Joseph realised it could only stay like that while his parents were getting better. Now that they were better, things had to change. Joseph also felt devastated by the way he felt, and didn't want to hurt his parents.

> Joseph's foster carer thought about how to support his moving on – it would be unfair to keep him in foster care, but Joseph's fears were important and should be kept in mind while planning the move. So the move happened slowly, with gradually increasing periods of contact with his parents. Joseph was kept informed of how his parents would continue to be supported. Joseph's old school would create a safe space for him with the learning mentor, who could monitor how Joseph was coping and would in any case see and talk with his parents as social services withdrew.
>
> The foster carer also wrote Joseph a letter after he had returned to his parents. In it, he described how much he appreciated Joseph's qualities: his strength and sensitivity, and how sensible he was to have given such important issues so much thought. The foster carer reminded Joseph in the letter that she was glad that Joseph had been happy in her home, and that he had done something that was really grown up – he cared for his own happiness, which is really important.

Short-term placements

Looked after children in short-term, bridging or emergency placements may experience the uncertainties of moving on without the supportive 'solid ground' of a familiar home environment.

Foster carers should be guided by the importance of the following themes:

- *welcoming* the young person

- *accepting* the young person

- *'holding'*

- *preparing* the young person to move on.

Many looked after children have experienced an impoverished welcome into the world from birth. The disruptions and placement moves will have an effect on the young person's growth – their personal development, academic development, physical and emotional well-being, as well as the spirit of the child – as their sense of hope is battered. Welcoming the young person and accepting them for who they are, even when it is difficult to understand their behaviour, is a crucial step, no matter how tiny, toward transforming their self-esteem and breaking patterns of poor attachments. (Chapters 4 and 5 explore these themes further.)

The word '**holding**' relates to when you experience a relationship where you feel able and confident about managing your distress. It is used here as a metaphor to draw attention to what it feels like to be emotionally 'held' with affection alone. Being held when you are in distress can be a comfort or reassuring. The feeling of being held can enable you to wind down and move on from the distress.

You may recall a time when you have felt held, metaphorically, within a conversation or, more generally, within a relationship. You may recall how *you* were comforted and reassured, or how you were helped to wind down and move on. Can you recall what happened, or what beliefs you had about the other person that enabled the experience of feeling held?

When thinking about how to *do* holding it is useful to refer to John Burnham's (1986) work on complementary relationships.

> An example is where one person is cared for and the other is carer, as with a client and therapist…these are referred to as the 'one-up' and 'one-down' positions respectively. Problems occur when a couple become entrenched in the relative positions. (p.12)

So taking a one-down position might mean allowing the other person to take a lead or to be more active than you.

Preparing the looked after child in a short-term placement for moving on is the fourth theme to guide the foster carer and is described above in 'bridging the difference'. Developing a complementary relationship will involve listening (or 'tuning in') to the child for when to take a one-down position; perhaps this will mean working out when to actually listen while the young person off-loads their distress, for example, and then when to intervene in the young person's off-loading from a one-up position and tell the young person that they are going to be okay and this is what we are going to do…

The task for the foster carer, as described above in 'bridging the difference', is to recall and apply what they have learnt about how children and young people accept gestures of comfort and reassurance, and also to give attention to their own beliefs around feeling comforted and reassured them-

selves, but to refer to those thoughts *lightly* and listen out for the unique perceptions and needs of the young person.

Long-term placements

Permanent placements present the looked after child with a different kind of
moving on: moving on from the uncertainty and disruption of transition to
that of certainty and the opportunity to settle down. In some instances the
short-term placement is converted into a long-term placement. However, in
the majority of cases, moving on to a permanent placement will also mean a
change in the young person's care relationship, as well as in their relationship to their birth family and the home and community it is linked to.

The birth family's relationship to the young person will also change.
The young person may notice a change but not understand it. These changes
may be confusing, welcomed or feared by the young person, and like most
experiences of change the move to a permanent placement may evoke a
mixture of thoughts and feelings. As with Joseph, the mixture is often conflicting and confusing. It is essential to talk and plan with the young person
prior to the move to a permanent placement, in the manner described above.
Contact between foster carers – the new, permanent placement foster carer
and the previous carer – will help to inform the whole bridging process.

It is important to address these issues of moving on to a permanent
placement. If conflicting thoughts and emotions are evoked in the change
and remain unresolved for too long, they will affect the mental health of the
young person, and the health (or healthy functioning) of the placement. A
deterioration in the health of the placement may cause it to become unsuit-
able or unsafe for the young person, and lead to a placement breakdown. A
looked after child may decide that deliberately breaking down the placement with intolerable behaviour is the way to restore some peace to the even
more intolerable distress they feel resulting from their conflicting thoughts,
feelings and allegiances.

Placement breakdowns

Foster carers can experience very strong emotions in the event of a
placement breakdown. They may set out to develop a feeling of near
normal family life that the looked after child can fit in to. If this does
not work foster carers can feel let down or betrayed by the young
person, or they may experience extreme disappointment in the

system of professional support, which they may believe is blaming
them for the breakdown of the placement. The task of caring for
looked after children can be a deceptively complex one; a task that
demands the foster carer to make a home for an exceptional young
person who has many layers of complex needs, behaviours, beliefs and
perceptions, so a placement breakdown will inevitably be a complex
event to make sense of, with many layers of reasons.

Although it may seem difficult for a foster carer with a mixture of
such strong feelings to remain within the young person's system of
care, it is important to pursue an assessment of the event – this can
be conducted with the link social worker. Both for the development of
the foster carer and their growing set of professional skills, abilities
and experience, and for the needs of the young person in the event of
a placement breakdown, the experience should be reflected on in
order to continue developing an understanding of how to support this
exceptional, unique and multi-layered young person.

If a complaint is made: moving on from difficulties

Whether within the context of a short-term or a longer-term placement,
when a child makes an allegation or complaint about a foster carer, the initial
impact on the carer can be devastating. They are overwhelmed by a mixture
of feelings including betrayal, violation and loss, and loss of dignity, authority and respect. In short, they feel much of what goes with being abused. The
parallel response to this devastating attack may be to reject the child in their
care and instigate an immediate end to the placement – if one has not been
previously arranged. At this point it is important to say that the foster carer's
feelings are absolutely valid, and perhaps are a provoked manifestation of
what the child carries with them from their past and into life today. While we
have made several references in this book to the difficulty for the *child* in
facing up to, and moving on from, experiences like this, foster carers cannot
reasonably anticipate fostering again unless they are able (with support) to
work through such breakdowns and the emotions they elicit, and 'move on'
themselves – with or without the child.

For allegations that are untrue, it takes a lot of patience and emotional
strength to look beyond the actual ordeal of the false allegation, and the
investigation that follows it, to what may be driving it. There is a complex
relationship between the child's previous experience of abuse and the recre-
ation of a quality of abuse between the child and the foster carer relationship.
One among the many layers of a young person who has experienced abuse

will carry a permanent imprint of it. For the abused or traumatised young person, their experience of abuse may have become normal and the foundation of the environment where they fitted in. Their beliefs about fitting in may shape how they actually 'do' the behaviour that they have come to understand as 'fitting in' to the foster placement. Child and Adolescent Mental Health Services (CAMHS) and the fostering agency can provide psychological therapy to support the foster carer's process of understanding and moving on from such events.

The foster carer's social worker will not be involved in investigating the allegation or complaint, and so will remain as a support for the carer in thinking through and making sense of the event in a way that facilitates an unhooking of the perception that this is a simple personal attack on the foster carer, their family, or their way of life.

We all have insecurities. Stressful events, such as having an allegation made against you, will touch on one's insecurities and self-doubts, and this can affect how you cope with the event and move on. Depersonalising an allegation can demand a great deal from a carer. The carer's network of support, friends and family, may feel unable to do anything but join in the rejection and demonising of an already abused child.

Leaving care

Children who leave the homes of their birth parents will generally leave at an older age, more mature in their development, and will also have a family and cultural history that will shape their beliefs about their continuing relationship with their parents – adult child to adult parent. Assumptions and expectations between the foster carer, young person leaving care and perhaps the young person's family will need to be negotiated or worked out openly. Many care leavers also struggle to cope with the practical, domestic realities of independent living. Whereas the average age for leaving home amongst the general population is around 22 years, the majority of looked after children leave care at 16 or 17 years. Leaving the care of a responsible adult is an immense step for children from stable homes, let alone those from foster homes, whose life may have been far more disrupted. When a child leaves a biological home they may well still perceive it as a safety net psychologically – somewhere. They can often rely on it to go back to. For young people who leave foster care this is not frequently the case, although there may be some continued contact. Although sad, it is very real for young people leaving foster care to re-experience self-doubts and critical feelings of self-worth. They may ask themselves questions such as 'If someone is not paid to look after me, will they be interested to help me in the future?', 'Who cares for me?', 'Who will be there for me in the future?'and 'Where do I belong, and who remembers me?'

When considering the psychological implications of moving on with regard to leaving the care system, it is important to consider the current lifestyle opportunities of care leavers and the (UK) legislative context for care leavers. The quality and achievements of the adult lives of people who have lived in care are wide-ranging and reflect their diversity as a group. However, a significant body of small-scale community-focused research with looked after children and social services departments completed through the 1980s and 1990s throughout the UK highlighted certain trends. The research showed the vulnerability of care leavers and their liability to experience isolation, depression, or one of a number of indicators of social exclusion.

- Eight to nine thousand young people leave care each year. Just under five thousand of them are aged 16 or 17 years. The majority of care leavers return to the care of their birth families; however, a large number of reunified families experience the process of repatriation as highly demanding and disruptive, but are reluctant to ask for local authority assistance (Department of Health 1999).

- Young adults who have been in care have historically been over-represented in UK prisons. The Howard League for Penal Reform (2005) research briefing showed that 24 per cent of the young men in prison who took part in the research had some experience of living in care.

- Biehal et al. (1995) reported that an estimated a quarter to a third of rough sleepers on London's streets had been in care.

- Of young women leaving care, 17 per cent are parents or are pregnant at the point of moving on to independent living from foster care.

- The majority of care leavers moving on to independent living will have no choice about their accommodation. The quality of accommodation offered to care leavers varies, as does the suitability of locations. Vulnerable young care leavers may risk the insecurity of hostel and bed-and-breakfast accommodation. Some locations will leave these most vulnerable young people exposed to prostitution and drug abuse (Department of Health 1999).

- The exam results of looked after children continue to compare poorly with the general population, with around three-quarters of care leavers attaining no qualifications at all. In addition to this, half of all care leavers who move to independent living have no job.

The UK Government has responded to research connecting care leavers and indicators of social exclusion by making changes to the Children Act (1989). The *Me, Survive, Out There?* consultation document (Department of Health 1999) led to the Children (Leaving Care) Act 2000. Both documents set out to build on the duties of children's services to looked after children beyond 16 and up to 21 years of age. The legislative background for care leavers since the mid-1970s has been that of increasing the visibility of care leavers as a vulnerable minority, and increasing the availability of professional support for them. The prospect of moving on and leaving care at 16 years of age or over, with the possibility of independent living, or leaving care and returning to the birth family, can carry with it all of the hopes and fears of previously discussed situations for moving on, with the addition of freedom from the authoritative face of the **corporate parent**. The mixture of feelings that young people often have churns away, ultimately producing the defiant urge to finally do what *they* want.

Foster carers may experience this as many parents experience their own children flying the nest, with all of the fearful pride that accompanies the event. However, the need for ritual (marking the event), planning, talking and also acknowledging the change in your relationship is incredibly important for care leavers. Again, the foster carer's link social worker can support the foster carer in planning and undertaking these conversations.

References

Biehal, N., Clayden, J., Stein, M. and Wade, J. (1995) *Moving On: Young People and Leaving Care Schemes.* London: HMSO.

Burnham, J.B. (1986) *Family Therapy.* London and New York: Routledge.

Department of Health (1999) *Me, Survive, Out There? New Arrangements for Young People Living in and Leaving Care.* London: The Stationery Office.

Howard League for Penal Reform (2005) *Young, neglected and back: young men in prison. Research briefing: 2.* London: Howard League for Penal Reform.

CHAPTER 11

Thinking Ahead

Social services departments have regular media campaigns to attract potential foster carers. They tend to advertise in local and national papers, have poster promotions, and even go on local radio to talk about fostering. However, many foster carers develop an interest from having personal contact with foster carers as friends or family.

By now, you will probably be feeling optimism mixed with slight worries about going further with your ideas of becoming a foster carer. Indeed, we have been very careful to present a balanced view of the extremely important and high profile role of a foster carer in modern society.

This chapter will focus on telling you about the process of assessing individuals, couples and families as potential foster carers. It is also a useful guide for existing foster carers who are undergoing a review.

Assessing foster carers

Foster carer assessments are carried out by social services departments and independent (private) fostering agencies. The process is governed by the Children Act 1989, but each agency will probably have a slightly different approach in the way they go about doing the assessment.

From expressing interest to actually being registered as a foster carer entails a lengthy process. This can lead to some feelings of tension.

Anxiety around the assessment process

It is important not to assume that the time it takes to assess a foster carer is a reflection of some inadequacy in the organisation or in your family. It would be more useful to monitor how you feel at different stages of this process, using a ten-point scale: for example, 0 = 'I feel

---

relaxed and confident' to 10 = 'I feel like giving up'. At the end of the assessment, look back at your overall scores. This is useful because your scores tell you about your capacity for coping with anxiety and frustration. This is very important feedback, as it will be a self-reflection of whether or not you will feel able to manage these common feelings of frustration and anxiety when you have an actual foster child in placement. If you often felt like giving up, this may be an indication that fostering will be a huge challenge to you and that you will need a relatively high level of support from your support network. Armed with this knowledge, you will be able to work with the agency to ensure that a solid system of support is established if you are registered.

Stage 1

You are likely to make telephone contact initially. After a brief chat with one of the social workers, you will probably get a visit from the assessor to obtain some basic information about you, such as your current employment and health status, your accommodation and your current family arrangements, and also to discuss your impressions of fostering. In this first discussion take the opportunity to ask as many questions as you can about what it involves and how the assessment is made. Commonly asked questions are:

- What are you looking for in a foster carer?

- Will I have to give up work?

- Will we be able to choose the children who come to live with us?

- Will I be told why the child is coming into foster care?

- What kind of support will I get to help me?

- How long will the assessment take?

Stage 2

The assessor will also inform you about the 'preparation groups' that have an important role in letting you know about all that fostering involves. There is usually a series of meetings over several weeks that you are expected to attend. They will be run both in the daytime and also in the evenings to accommodate people who are working full-time. You will get a chance to meet other people who are interested in fostering, and you will also be able to meet experienced foster carers and specialists in child development and child care. Your attendance and contribution may form part of your assessment. After this series of meetings you will usually be asked to think, together with your family and/or your support network, about whether you should go on to the next stage of the assessment.

It is hugely important that you carefully consider before going on to the next stage of what will become a major transformation in your life and in the lives of everyone in your household.

Stage 3

Once the organisation receives confirmation that you would like to continue with the assessment, you will be contacted by an assessor to commence a series of interviews and observations with you and the other members of your household. You will be seen both individually and together. It is useful to see this stage of the process as a two-way assessment. You will be able to gain information on whether fostering will really suit you and your family, and you will also gain a sense of how you and your family may be supported by the organisation when you talk about times that were difficult for you to parent, or when you were a child. This is because you can directly ask the organisation what kind of support they may be able to give or obtain for you to deal with similar problems, should they arise when you are caring for a foster child. The interviews will ask about your experiences of being parented and/or being a parent, as well as asking you about significant relationships in your past and present, your lifestyle and your attitudes to issues such as diversity (in terms of, for example, sexuality, **ethnicity**, religious practices, etc.). You will have an opportunity to say what children you would feel more comfortable and confident to foster, taking into account, for example, physical disability, sexually abuse, age range, gender, etc. The assessor will use all of this information to highlight your strengths and abilities, but also to pinpoint where and how you are likely to need crucial support as a foster carer. The assessor will also interview people whom you put forward as referees to comment on your potential as a foster carer.

Stage 4

Many people have never had cause to make contact with the police or criminal justice system. For many foster carers the idea of asking a sibling or even an elderly parent to consent to a police check will appear as an intolerable breach of their privacy. Some relatives may find the mere act of having a check on their past or their character very threatening indeed. A single process, such as a police check can trigger foster carers' associations with earlier assessments, or other processes, that made public what was once their private and personal information.

Foster carers will have few choices around these issues as safety for everyone taking part in the foster caring system (the carer, the carer's family and the fostered child) will inevitably outweigh considerations of personal privacy. What foster carers can do is make use of their own social worker to discuss the issues, so as to arrive at a comfortable enough balance and understanding of how to reconcile the safety and privacy in a way that is enabling for them.

Statutory checks – who? what? why? when? A sample of compulsory checks made by fostering agencies

- *Enhanced Criminal Records Bureau* (CRB) *disclosure* – All applicants and persons aged 16 years or over living in the household need to have a satisfactory enhanced CRB disclosure. This has to be repeated every three years.

- *Employer reference* – Your current or most recent employer has to be contacted by letter.

- *Local authority checks* – All local authorities hold a database that will be able to provide information on the family's history of contact with the areas where they have taken up residence.

- *General practitioner* – Your GP will be asked to confirm that you are mentally and physically fit to foster. Long-term and kinship carers have to have a full medical examination, and an agency medical adviser will comment on the report from the examination.

- *School* – If there are children resident in the home who are of statutory school age, their school will be asked to write a summary of the family's contact with the school.

- *Health visitor* – If there are children aged under five years living in the household, then their health visitor will be asked to write a summary of the family's contact with them.

- *Personal references* – A minimum of four people (six if there is no employer reference or school or health visitor details available) should be put forward to provide personal references. They

> must have known the applicant over a period covering the
> previous ten years. Three of these references will be followed up
> with face-to-face interviews by the assessing social worker.
>
> • *OFSTED* – If you have a history of childminding, the database held
>   by OFSTED will be checked to provide a summary of your status
>   as a childminder.
>
> • *Ex-partners* – Previous significant partners (marriage, co-habited
>   or children together) will be contacted and asked for their views
>   on the applicant's suitability.
>
> (Source: Luton Borough Council Children and Families Division 2006)

Stage 5

The information for the interviews will be transferred to a legal document
called a 'Form F'. It is the official assessment form to be completed by the
assessor and presented to a panel of people who consider the suitability of
foster carers. In addition to the information from the interviews, the assessor
is legally obliged to complete a range of compulsory checks on the people in
the household – this will be on your medical status, criminal history,
employment and financial status, and the physical condition of your home.
The assessor will then summarise on the form:

- your understanding, attitudes and ideas about fostering and the
  varying needs and behaviour of foster children

- your parenting abilities and your family's capability to support a
  foster child

- your lifestyle and any associated financial and health issues

- what financial, social and professional support you are likely to
  need or use

- your attitudes to seeking help and working with other agencies,
  especially schools.

Form F cannot be submitted to this panel without you first having an opportunity to read and comment on it and to sign that you agree with its contents.

Stage 6

The membership of the foster panel is prescribed in the Children Act 1989. They are usually made up of local practitioners with specialist knowledge and interest in fostering, as well as a registered foster carer and an ex-foster child. The panel meets regularly to recommend and review foster carers on behalf of the local authority. The assessor will encourage you to attend this panel with them, as this is a strong symbol of your intent to cooperate with the fostering organisation. The meeting is usually for the adults in the household, and therefore they do not expect you to bring your children with you to this meeting. The panel is very aware of how nerve-racking this meeting can be for potential foster carers, and usually tries very hard to put you at ease and to encourage you to make any further points that you want to make. The panel will usually ask you and your assessor to clarify any issues that remain unclear from Form F. They will then decide whether they would recommend you and/or your family for registration as foster carers. The final decision is made by the senior managers of the fostering organisation, for example director of social services (who may delegate this task to an assistant director), or the managing director of an independent fostering agency.

Stage 7

You are usually informed of the panel's decision by letter. If the decision is 'Yes, we would like to recommend that you are registered as a foster carer', you will probably be elated. You will still, however, have the opportunity to reconsider whether you wish to complete the registration process, before confirming that you would indeed like to go forward for registration.

From time to time the panel asks the assessor to obtain further information from yourself or other members of your household, or from referees, or from the compulsory checks, and inform you that once they are satisfied with the information that is returned to them they will recommend your registration to the fostering organisation.

In very rare circumstances, the panel does not recommend that someone should register as a foster carer at this stage. Rejection raises powerful emotions that link in to other negative emotions, such as disappointment, loss, bereavement, grief, anger, shame and guilt. It will also put you in touch with 'buried' emotions from memories of unhappy events in your past. Once you have picked yourself up off the floor, muster the courage to read the letter again. It should give clear and concise reasons why they decided not to recommend you on this occasion. It may be to do with some issue that you feel can be discussed further. However, there are sometimes other reasons outside of your direct control, for example the age and needs of your own children. Whatever the reasons given, you do have the right to appeal. The letter giving the panel's decision will explain what you need to do next if you decide to appeal against their decision. You can discuss your intention to appeal with the assessor. Whatever you decide to do about an appeal, you may re-apply in the future, if and when your situation changes.

Self-assessment

Below is a scale that you can use as a tool for providing feedback to you and your family/household about your knowledge, skills, and understanding of fostering and the specific needs of foster children. It will give you direct feedback on areas that you can find out more about, both before and after embarking on the journey towards registering as a foster carer.

SELF-ASSESSMENT QUESTIONNAIRE

There is a questionnaire template for you to photocopy in Appendix B. More specific ones are given at the end of the chapter.

Complete the questionnaire:

1.   at the beginning of the application process and

2.   at the end of your assessment.

You can ask your partner and/or your children to complete one for themselves, or you can complete the questionnaire according to your **perception** of their knowledge and understanding.

Shade in the boxes that correspond to your perception of your knowledge of the areas specified.

Burnout

Once you have been registered, self-assessment in relation to monitoring your own stress levels or thresholds of tolerance will be a vital part of providing an emotionally safe environment – not just for foster children, but also for your own children. Inevitably when carers are caught up in the everyday routines of life and managing their range of relationships (and the duties and hopes that seem to just come with the roles of foster carer, parent, partner, son or daughter…) it can be difficult to take a step back in order to think through and understand the intricacy of the caring relationship, its impact on the foster carer, and why one fostering relationship may give rise to more preoccupation than another.

Feelings of guilt and failure can cast a shadow over all of the efforts of the foster carer if their capacity to continue as before within their own significant system (with their children, partner, parents) appears to evaporate in the face of the demands of the fostered child or children. These feelings may be fleeting. However, if they remain they may begin to characterise the foster carer's own perception of their ability, and may also lead to a kind of **burnout** or emotional exhaustion.

Shared care, with responsibility for the looked after child's care split between the birth family and foster carers, can lead the foster carers to develop a supportive relationship with the birth parent or parents, as caring for the child will demand a harmonisation of styles, expectations and boundary setting. This arrangement can lead the foster carer to embark on at least as intricate and demanding a range of relationships as with full care, and sometimes also to the same kind of burnout.

The most important thing that foster carers can do to avoid burnout is to make use of their supervising social worker, and also to make supportive connections with other foster carers through support groups or coffee mornings. Sharing experiences can help carers to reconnect to their own particular skills and qualities. Social services and fostering agencies will provide training and further opportunities to meet with other carers. **Respite** should be planned into the household routine and should not be mistaken for a sign of lack of robustness on the part of the foster carer, or badness in the fostered child/children. Social services can arrange respite with other carers, or perhaps a relative of the foster carer, following a police check, can provide a more 'normal' provision, as 'respite' can then be translated as 'staying overnight with (extended) family'.

Reference

Luton Borough Council Children and Families Division (2006) *Foster Carers' Handbook 2006*. Luton: Luton Borough Council.

At the beginning of the assessment

What I already know about foster children from my experience			
	Firm knowledge	Developing knowledge	Weak or no knowledge
Adolescence			
Behaviour problems			
Bereavement and loss			
Diversity			
Drug/alcohol abuse			
Education			
Emotional problems			
Learning difficulties			
Physical impairments			
Sensory impairments			
Separation from families			
Sexually abused children			
Stress and distress (trauma) in children			
Youth offending			

What my partner (or children) have learnt from the assessment process			
	Firm knowledge	Developing knowledge	Weak or no knowledge
Adolescence			
Behaviour problems			
Bereavement and loss			
Diversity			
Drug/alcohol abuse			
Education			
Emotional problems			
Learning difficulties			
Physical impairments			
Sensory impairments			
Separation from families			
Sexually abused children			
Stress and distress (trauma) in children			
Youth offending			

At the end of the assessment

What I have learnt about foster children from reading and training			
	Firm knowledge	Developing knowledge	Weak or no knowledge
Adolescence			
Behaviour problems			
Bereavement and loss			
Diversity			
Drug/alcohol abuse			
Education			
Emotional problems			
Learning difficulties			
Physical impairments			
Sensory impairments			
Separation from families			
Sexually abused children			
Stress and distress (trauma) in children			
Youth offending			

What my partner (or children) have learnt from the assessment process			
	Firm knowledge	Developing knowledge	Weak or no knowledge
Adolescence			
Behaviour problems			
Bereavement and loss			
Diversity			
Drug/alcohol abuse			
Education			
Emotional problems			
Learning difficulties			
Physical impairments			
Sensory impairments			
Separation from families			
Sexually abused children			
Stress and distress (trauma) in children			
Youth offending			

CHAPTER 12

Conclusion

In introducing this book we described it as a 'guide'. This is an important word in describing what we hoped to achieve in putting our writings together, with foster care professionals and foster carers specifically in mind as our readers.

We have presented some information, particularly in describing the legislative issues, and issues around diagnosis. These are things which we can commonly refer to as 'knowing' or not knowing. Alongside this information we have attempted to guide you along other pathways of understanding to discover a 'knowing' and meaning which are ultimately much more subjective, much more fluid and personal. There are many ways of 'knowing' things, and the psychological 'sciences' and therapies present us with a complex and sometimes contradictory playground of theories and ideas with which to explore knowing. Most important, we hope we have presented the idea that self-knowing, and knowing-in-relation-to-others (the idea of discovering who you are, and who others are, in the course of a relationship), is an ongoing and critical part of working intimately with other humans who are vulnerable and confused.

Each of the authors regularly provides consultations to foster carers, and we have attempted to examine here some of the issues that arise most frequently in such consultations. But there are 'umbrella' themes which encompass the individual consultations and pervade the nature of them all. Two of these themes are linked in this book, and we think it is important to summarise them in this conclusion. The two themes are **professionalisation** of foster care and the protective shield.

We are genuine in our belief that foster care stands at the crux of at least two streams of feeling and thinking about what looked after children need. The first stream is that looked after children need 'expert' help. This suggests that foster carers should be in this mix of 'expertise' in the care they offer the children. The second stream is that the children need 'families', which suggests that foster carers provide the combination of fallibility, humanity and intimacy that all humans need to grow up well. To do either 'expertise' or 'family' very well would be exceptional; to do both simultaneously well would be perhaps almost impossible. Perhaps 'expertise' and 'professional-ism' should not be understood in the very limited way that they can sometimes be taken, and certainly not as fixed ideas, but relative to the circumstances. We believe the concept of 'professional' foster care should always imply a deeply felt humanity combined with an understanding of the optimum contribution to be made to the child's life in professional relations with other colleagues. Understanding the role of fostering in relation to being part of a 'joined-up' service – as part of this shield – allows each part of the shield to negotiate and best fulfil its role in relation to the individual child. So for child 'A' the foster carer may provide the best possible service to the child by being a safe haven from all the assessments and 'treatments', but for child 'B' the foster carer may need to be much more active in behavioural management.

We believe the protective shield provides the best model for understand-ing how to meet the needs of troubled looked after children. It is an adapt-able idea with many layers which can help all those concerned with the child to consider the child's individual best interests at any one point in time, like a review meeting, and how the component parts of the shield fit together and work together, or don't.

Confidence in one's own role is only part of the story, however, and often in this book we have hoped to present information to foster carers that helps to sustain their confidence, ability and **resilience** in relation to the child and themselves, and also helps them to understand and feel more con-fident about others' role in the protective shield. This confidence helps the shield to 'glue together' better, and there is a less risk that gaping holes will leave the child unprotected.

We can say, then, that foster care provides the touchstone of care for the child, and that in carrying out this role the foster carers have incredible responsibility – but most certainly not sole responsibility: they cannot, and should not, have to try to be 'everything' and do everything.

Any child needs a great deal of care and can, at times, drain the resources of one or two parents easily. Looked after children can be expected to more consistently tire those parenting them. In this book we have suggested in many ways the amount of self-care that needs to be observed when fostering, and the variety of ways in which this can be done – via the protective shield in sharing responsibilities, via the extended family and community, etc. In our consultations we find there is a linked train of thought that leads to foster carers often *not* taking care. First, because somehow they do not value what they do as foster carers, and this can often be experienced as others (like social workers, therapists, etc.) not valuing them. Second, because they do not experience the system, or protective shield as it has been presented here, taking responsibility, so that they feel they must 'fill the gaps' themselves.

The end result is often that both foster carer and child feel alienated and abandoned, and this dynamic is not helpful. Certainly part of our message in this book has been to assert a right to respect and support for both parties – the foster carer and the child – but also to emphasise that *only the foster carer can be relied upon to notice when feelings like this arise, and insist on help to help the child.* The child is like a river, and he or she is busy *being* a river – turbulent and noisy at some stages, quiet and still and without energy at other stages. The foster carer has one foot in this river, but needs another on the bank. This other foot provides important grounding and distance to notice what is happening and intervene directly or indirectly when appropriate.

We hope that the book has opened up opportunities for you to explore thoughts, feelings and ideas, and that you have found it useful in your journey to, and through, fostering.

UNICEF Article 20

The UN Convention on the Rights of the Child (1990)

1. A child temporarily or permanently deprived of his or her family environment, or in whose own best interests cannot be allowed to remain in that environment, shall be entitled to special protection and assistance provided by the State.

2. State parties shall in accordance with their national laws ensure alternative care for such a child.[1]

3. Such care should include, *inter alia*, foster placement, *kafalah* of Islamic law, adoption, or, if necessary, placement in suitable institutions for the care of children. When considering solutions, due regard shall be paid to the desirability of continuity in a child's upbringing and to the child's ethnic, religious, cultural and linguistic background.

This Article suggests a hierarchy of placement options for a child separated from family and neighbourhood, placing foster care before adoption and residential care. The earlier declaration on social and legal principles relating to the protection and welfare of children (UN 1986) contains specific guidance on foster care and adoption. For example it states that:

---

1   In some Islamic countries, particularly in the Middle East and South East Asia, adoption is considered to contradict their religious doctrine. Instead, a permanent form of fostering is promoted called *kafalah*. Within *kafalah* foster care is a service that supports birth family care or one that completely substitutes for that care. In these Islamic countries supplementary foster care is generally a short-term service for families and children to assist them in overcoming a temporary crisis often related to parental absence through illness or imprisonment or where the children have been or are likely to be harmed. Substitute foster care will involve a longer period of alternative care for children who cannot be cared for by their parents because of death, loss, maltreatment or long-term illness.

- workers responsible for foster placements should have appropriate professional training

- the placement of children should be regulated by law

- foster care should not preclude either family reunification or adoption

- in all matters foster carers and, as appropriate, the children and parents should be properly involved

- the placement should be supervised by a competent authority or agency to ensure the child's welfare.

Reference

UN (1986) *Declaration on Social and Legal Principles Relating to the Protection and Welfare of Children, with Special Reference to Foster Placement and Adoption Nationally and Internationally.* Commission of Human Rights.

Self-assessment Questionnaire

Tick the box that best illustrates your knowledge about these areas:

	Firm knowledge	Developing knowledge	Weak or no knowledge
Adolescence			
Behaviour problems			
Bereavement and loss			
Diversity			
Drug/alcohol abuse			
Education			
Emotional problems			
Learning difficulties			
Physical impairments			
Sensory impairments			
Separation from families			
Sexually abused children			
Stress and distress (trauma) in children			
Youth offending			

Glossary

actualise/actualisation A term used to describe the growth and development in the course of one's life towards realising potential.

analytic psychology A theory of the mind derived from and including Carl Gustav Jung's conceptualisation of human behaviour that relates the life of the individual to the collective or universal unconscious.

appropriate adult This is the description given to the adult who has responsibility for a child's well-being. This adult will change according to the setting that the child is in, but relates to the foster carer if the child requires representation and support in school or other formal settings, as delegated by the child's social worker.

attuned A state of being that occurs when someone is able to perceive, understand and respond to someone's needs and feelings. You might feel this when you deeply understand what someone is going through and you 'instinctively' say/do the 'right' thing at the right time. Being attuned relates to a state of harmony (as in music) and is often to do with sensing unexpressed emotions.

behavioural theory, behavioural therapy A psychological theory of learning (called conditioning) that describes the way in which people can be taught to change their behaviour by altering the events that occur before (antecedents) or after the behaviour takes place (reinforcers). It is likely that you would have been taught about reinforcers as 'positive', such as a reward (e.g. special time and attention), and 'negative', such as a punishment (e.g. 'time-out'). Behavioural therapy is based on these principles and the therapist is active in exploring with the client the precise antecedents and reinforcers that maintain the behaviour that the client wishes to change.

bias Used here to describe how a person or test might be inclined towards something, or prejudiced towards something or someone. Some statistical tests try and eliminate any possible bias so that the results are more objective.

bully–victim cycle This is when a victim reaches a point where they feel that the only way to protect themselves is to go on the offensive. This may show itself as making the first 'strike' in order to avoid being in a position of feeling defenceless. Observers will then see a person who looks as though they are the person who is always making the first attack. It can also be seen as developing over several years, where a person develops a strategy for managing conflict that fits with the idea of 'harm or be harmed'.

burnout Involves emotional and physical elements of exhaustion and a sense of being unable to cope in a way previously experienced. The term is typically applied to those in the caring professions who fail to listen to signs from their own bodies and emotions that they need a break. Often this might happen because they feel they must put others' well-being before their own.

CAMHS Sometimes called 'CAM-H'; the Child and Adolescent Mental Health Service. A National Health Service (NHS) provision.

cognitive Relating to the mind and the thinking/perceptual processes that are carried out.

cognitive therapies A process of change that involves the active exploration of the thoughts and beliefs that the client holds that potentially contribute to the maintenance of the behaviour that the client wishes to change.

contact Social services and parents should work out how a looked after child remains in contact with parents or anyone with parental responsibility, relatives and friends.

contained/containment Words are used here in the sense that they are used in therapeutic 'language'. The theory suggests that as we grow and learn we also learn to be able to tolerate difficult feelings – we quite literally 'contain' them, in the sense that we do let them 'spill out' inappropriately. Feeling contained when young (i.e. an adult is able to tolerate your feelings for you and manage them appropriately) is thought to help you develop this capacity yourself. Linked to **regulation**.

corporate parent 'Parent' is used deliberately to remind children's services of the overall nature of their obligations and duties toward children in public care.

counselling A form of talking therapy that is designed to support people in processing their feelings of confusion and/or unhappiness.

disclosure The revelation of an experience that had previously been kept secret.

emotional abuse (*also known as: verbal abuse, mental abuse, and psychological maltreatment*) Includes acts or the failures to act by parents or caretakers that have caused, or could cause, serious behavioural, cognitive, emotional or mental disorders. This can include parents/caretakers using extreme and/or bizarre forms of punishment, such as confinement in a closet or dark room, or being tied to a chair for long periods of time, or threatening or terrorising a child. Less severe acts, but no less damaging, are belittling or rejecting treatment, using derogatory terms to describe the child, and habitual scapegoating or blaming.

empathic The ability to let oneself get close to another person's felt experience. Empathy is not necessarily to sympathise.

EP Educational psychologist.

esteem The general result of how one judges or regards one's self.

ethnicity A group connected by a common cultural tradition and sense of identity. Language, faith, history and locality may each serve to define an ethnic group. Ethnic groups are sometimes racial, but not exclusively.

EWO Educational welfare officer. A professional employed by the school or LEA with particular responsibilities for monitoring and supporting the attendance and punctuality of children to school.

existential counselling and psychotherapy Existentialism is a philosophy that was developed in Europe in the last half of the twentieth century. Its main idea is related to how we go about asking and answering questions about the meaning of our individual existence –

what it means to 'live' before we die. Existential counselling and psychotherapy is about assisting individuals in that process of understanding and making sense of their life. It is distinct from other types of psychotherapy because it emphasises that the meaning of each person's life can only be determined by the individual. This is because only the individual truly understands what it is like to be themselves. It emphasises the uniqueness of each individual, and therefore supports the individual in asking and answering questions that evaluate who they see themselves as today. Existential psychotherapy will not necessarily expect you to focus on your childhood but more on the combination of your entire life experiences, how you perceived them at the time, and how you learned from or believe you were changed by your life experiences. At the heart of existential psychotherapy and counselling is also the idea that life is 'bittersweet' and will be filled with both painful and pleasant experiences and both of these are equally valid. For example, it is a common fantasy for people in Western societies that a wealthy person has fewer painful experiences because they have a lot of money, when the reality is that they are just as likely to experience, say, a bereavement (and the pain, grief, loss and depression of it) as anyone else.

family therapy   A social psychological approach to therapy. Family therapists traditionally meet with families in order to address problems between family members and the relational causes of emotional distress. More and more often family therapists are working with a growing diversity of social groups and organisations. Influenced largely by **systemic** theory, family therapists are coming to be known as systemic psychotherapists.

genogram   A visual tool used within a number of professions, including family therapy, to show, as a picture, the system of relationships that make a family. Like family trees, genograms can be used to map bloodlines, to tell a family history or to show how traditions are repeated generation after generation.

group management   The art of using one's knowledge and skills in observing group dynamics and interpersonal communication to enhance the effectiveness of that group. This is a common task for teachers and for others who are responsible for ensuring that a group is harmonious in its communication and problem-solving abilities.

guardian ad litem   A legal representative appointed to a child by the courts.

holding   A very broadly used term in the psychological professions that has much meaning. Here it is used to describe in short term the experience of being able to contain (mainly psychologically) difficult and powerful feelings within oneself, or work with someone in a way that encourages such holding or **containment**. It is thought that this is something that may be learned from very early years, and that physical closeness and bonding with the mother has a role in helping an infant develop the capacity to hold/contain themselves in later years.

holistic   Used to describe an approach to thinking about an individual as both a biological and a social being, and therefore taking into account the combined influences of their physical and emotional health, as well as factors in their social environment, for example family, friendships, neighbourhood, work, school, etc.

humanism   Otherwise known as the Human Potential Movement. Developed through the 1960s initially as a critical response to **psychoanalysis**.

identity   What constitutes a person.

instinct   Used in Chapter 4 to denote a basic biological/genetic need (like feeding) that can be assumed to be present from birth.

instinctual A way of reacting/thinking/feeling that relies seemingly more on instinct than on more conscious, logical processes. The idea of 'instinctual' relies to some degree on the idea that we are 'intelligent' at a basic, emotional level and that it is helpful if we can recognise this and act on these feelings sometimes.

internalising In this book this term is meant to convey the idea that we all 'translate' our external perception of events into internal meaning(s). How we 'internalise' experience is always unique, although some typical patterns can sometimes be seen: the adage of those who tend towards pessimism in their basic character as always 'seeing the glass as half empty' may be a simple example. Chapter 4 (on relationships) talks more about internalisation.

joined-up working The authors know this phrase most in connection with lessons learnt in past social services inquiries from failures to protect children. A frequent feature of the failure of services to protect children has been the inadequacy of their communication to each other about the child. The term 'joined-up working' therefore relates to the idea that services share information about a child, work cooperatively to secure the best interests of the child, and work together to enable open/cooperative systems more generally. The idea of the 'protective shield' encompasses this philosophy of how best to provide services to secure the child's best interests.

latent Something that is there, but maybe not in an active sense. For example, someone may have a tendency to a particular viral infection – like warts – but it needs something else, like ill health, for it to appear. The viral infection is always present, but is latent, until something else provides the conditions where it might appear.

marginalisation The process of moving away from a central or majority position within a group or community.

neglect The failure to provide for the child's basic needs. Neglect can be physical, educational or emotional. Physical neglect can include failure to provide adequate food or clothing, appropriate medical care, supervision, or proper weather protection (hat or coats). It may include abandonment. Educational neglect includes failure to provide appropriate schooling or special educational needs, or allowing excessive truancies. Psychological neglect includes the lack of any emotional support and love, never attending to the child, spousal abuse, and drug and alcohol abuse (including allowing the child to participate in drug and alcohol use).

neural pathways 'Highways' in the brain carrying information from one part of the nervous system to another part.

neuroscience The scientific study of the nervous system (brain, etc.).

non-conscious Not readily available to awareness although some elements of non-conscious knowing can be recalled or discovered at times. Non-conscious is used in Chapter 4 as preferable to 'unconscious'.

paediatrician A medical doctor who specialises in the ailments of children.

perception The process of understanding what we see, hear, smell, taste and feel.

pervasive A term often used in relation to mental health or psychological problems/difficulties that have a tendency to affect all areas of functioning and often be longer term and sometimes difficult to treat.

physical abuse The inflicting of physical injury upon a child. This may include burning, hitting, punching, shaking, kicking, beating, or otherwise harming a child. The parent or caretaker may not have intended to hurt the child, but the injury is not an accident. It may, however, have been the result of over-discipline or physical punishment that is inappropriate to the child's age.

preverbal   Occurring before language is acquired.

process management   The art of using one's knowledge of the potential impact of inter-personal communication on the problem-solving process. The art of process management will mean that one should be able to use both verbal and nonverbal communication to provide ef-fective feedback to keep the problem-solving process moving along towards a full resolution. Although commonly associated with **group management**, good process management skills can also be evident in a one-to-one setting.

professionalisation   A term coined to explain the progression towards training foster carers to develop their skills as specialist child care practitioners, and to build careers in this area of expertise.

psyche   The psychological structure of a person.

psychiatry   The body of information available from the medical study of mental and emotional processes and the environmental, social, biochemical and physiological influences on these processes.

psychoanalysis   The body of theory and practices derived from and including Sigmund Freud's conceptualisation of human behaviour.

psychology   The body of information available from the social scientific study of the behaviour of humans and animals. Sometimes the term is used as an abbreviation to describe the mental, emotional and social processes associated with an individual's behaviour.

psycho-social   A short term for 'psychological and social'. In the term there is implied the impact that social factors have on psychological issues, and vice versa. Hence we may say that the psycho-social implications of depression might be low mood and isolation, etc.

psychosomatic   From **psyche**, *mind / mental processes*, and somatic, *bodily*. A psychosomatic condition will have connecting mind and body symptoms.

psychosis   A mental illness in which thinking and emotion are so disturbed that the person may be seriously out of contact with what is commonly described as reality.

regulation   Linked with **containment**. Engines regulate themselves – as in car engines and the coolant system. People also regulate themselves in a number of ways – bodily, mentally, etc. Regulation of emotions has been linked to a learned capacity for this: for example, a baby who is left to cry for a while but is then soothed experiences the bodily and emotional tension of crying and the relief and calming of being soothed. Theory suggests that that baby will grow up with a better capacity for tolerating and managing emotions such as anger and despair, and will better regulate these feelings for itself.

reparative   A relationship or act which helps to heal psychological 'wounds'.

representation   An individual's way of understanding in their own mind what is presented to them. A drawing could be said to be one kind of representation, but psychology also helps us understand how most 'things' are represented in different ways to different individuals. To one a banana might represent being 'good to yourself' and eating healthily. To another it might be hard to look at a banana without remembering that they were forced to eat them as a child, and now they hate them, and they hate being forced to do anything, etc. We all have very individual reactions to things and events around us and these reactions might be partly determined by the representations we have about them.

resilience   The personal strength to manage adversity.

respite   A period of change, rest or recuperation between periods of stay with a main carer.

Rogerian   Carl Rogers developed the Rogerian idea that we each have at our core a kind of animal or free nature that knows how to thrive, a 'whole' person. However, the events and expectations of living have put our true natures into a kind of sleep. The process of awakening involves making honest contact with our selves through emotions and sensuality rather than intellect. (Kovel, J. 1991)

SENCo   A school's Special Educational Needs Co-ordinator.

sexual abuse   Inappropriate sexual behaviour with a child. It includes fondling a child's genitals, making the child fondle the adult's genitals, intercourse, incest, rape, sodomy, exhibitionism and sexual exploitation. To be considered child abuse these acts have to be committed by a person responsible for the care of a child (for example a baby-sitter, a parent, or a daycare provider), or related to the child. If a stranger commits these acts, it is considered sexual assault and handled solely by the police and criminal courts.

Commercial or other exploitation of a child relates to use of the child in work or other activities for the benefit of others. This includes, but is not limited to, child labour and child prostitution. These activities are to the detriment of the child's physical or mental health, education, or spiritual, moral or social-emotional development.

significant harm   A term which was 'coined' mainly with the 1989 Children Act. The exact definition of significant harm was not spelt out in the Act because it is a term that must be applied in context – that is, to the specific child in the specific circumstances at the specific time, etc. However, common sense indicates that harm that is 'significant' is noteworthy and in some way out of the anticipated norm. It is one of the threshold criteria for deciding if a child should be removed from the home.

social construction   An approach to making sense of human life/existence. Social constructionists are interested in what individuals do and say together and the rules we generate in order to coordinate with each other. They believe that it is this basic way of being social that ultimately generates our personal, cultural, political and historical realities.

socialised   Having had success in the process of learning to integrate and adapt to a social group/s.

standardised tests   These are tests used often by psychologists. They are felt to be very valuable because they have been carefully developed in steps so that they can be repeated by different people with different people, in different situations, over and over again in the same way, so that professionals can be more confident that the results of the tests reflect results that can be compared. Exams are a little like this: the same questions, given in the same way, test the person's knowledge in a way that can be compared to that of other people.

stereotype   An ultimately limited and standardised idea of an identifiable group.

stigmatisation   To threaten or mark a person's reputation.

stress   The emotional effect of being under sustained pressure, or of being overwhelmed.

subconscious   A name for a place in the mind where memories gather out of reach of our awareness.

systemic   Pearce and Walters (1996) describe the approach of systems thinking by drawing a distinction with the approach of science whose approach is, traditionally, to analyse the parts in isolation in order to develop an understanding of the whole; 'the intellectual move of "systems thinking" is to put things together and study how they are related' (p.14). This can be applied to people in the 'system' of a family or community.

thrive   To grow exceptionally well, or to flourish.

tracheostomy   A surgical procedure where a small hole is made through the skin and into the trachea (windpipe) to enhance the patient's ability to circulate air into their lungs. This procedure may require the regular use of a suction pump to remove the build-up of catarrh that becomes trapped in the hole.

transpersonal   Beyond the experience of the socialised individual – sometimes thought of as the spiritual.

trauma   A reaction to a life-threatening or terrifying event, the reaction to which goes on to interfere with a familiar continuation of everyday life.

validation   Being justified. Acceptance and approval.

visibility   What can be seen of a person, such as skin colour and dress. It also relates to beliefs that are expressed and made visible through a person's behaviour.

References

Kovel, J. (1991) *A Complete Guide to Therapy, from Psychoanalysis to Behaviour Modification.* New York: Pantheon Books. Hassocks, UK: Harvester Press. Reprinted by the Penguin Group.

Pearce, W.B. and Walters, K.A. (1996) *Research Methods: A Systemic Communication Approach. A Handbook for a Participatory Seminar in Research Methods.* Woodside, CA: PearceWalters, Inc.

Useful Resources

Afiya Trust www.afiya-trust.org
Aims to reduce health inequalities for people from racial groups.

Alcohol Concern www.alcoholconcern.org.uk

Antidote www.antidote.org.uk; tel. 020 7247 3355
Campaign for emotional literacy.

British Association of Social Workers www.basw.co.uk

British Deaf Association www.britishdeafassociation.org.uk

British Pregnancy Advisory Service www.bpas.org

Brook www.brook.org.uk/content/
Provides free and confidential sexual health advice and contraception for young people.

Bullying Online www.bullying.co.uk
Help and advice for parents and pupils.

Bullying Project www.bullying.org

Carers UK www.carersuk.org; tel. 020 7490 8818

Changing Minds www.rcpsych.ac.uk/campaigns/cminds
Aims to increase public awareness of mental health problems and reduce stigma.

Childline www.childline.org; tel. (helpline) 0800 1111

Children's Legal Centre www.childrenslegalcentre.com; tel. 01206 873820

Connexions www.connexions-direct.com
Information and advice for young people.

Depression Alliance www.depressionalliance.org
Support for those affected by depression and their carers.

Exam Aid tel. 01297 625982
Practical help for 10–13 year olds.

Frank www.talktofrank.com
An anonymous, discreet but well-informed friend. Frank will be ready to offer advice, information and support about drugs.

Internet Health Library www.internethealthlibrary.com

Mummy's Blue www.mummysblue.co.uk
Support and advice for post-natal depression.

NAFSIYAT 278 Seven Sisters Road, London N4 2HY
Intercultural therapy centre

National Association for the Care and Resettlement of Offenders (NACRO)
www.nacro.org

National Institute for Mental Health in England (NIMHE) www.nimhe.csip.org.uk

Pink Paper www.pinkpaper.com
News and events for the gay and lesbian community.

Puffta www.puffta.co.uk
Gay teens website.

Raising Kids www.raisingkids.co.uk
Free advice and information to parents.

Refugee Council Online www.refugeecouncil.org.uk
Provides up-to-date information for refugees and asylum seekers.

SCODA DrugScope www.ncvo-vol.org.uk/scoda

Terrence Higgins Trust www.tht.org.uk
Provides services and campaigns to promote good sexual health and reduce the spread of HIV.

Young Minds www.youngminds.org.uk
Campaigns to improve child mental health. Provides a parents' information service and a range of support services for children and professionals.

Index